W9-DFB-560

THE GLASS WALL

Why Mathematics Can Seem Difficult

FRANK SMITH

Teachers College, Columbia University
New York and London

Published by Teachers College Press, 1234 Amsterdam Avenue, New York, NY 10027

Library of Congress Cataloging-in-Publication Data

Smith, Frank, 1928–
The glass wall : why mathematics can seem difficult / Frank Smith.
p. cm.
Includes bibliographical references and index.
ISBN 0-8077-4242-2 (acid-free paper)—ISBN 0-8077-4241-4 (pbk. : acid-free paper)
1. Mathematics—Study and teaching. 2. Mathematics—Psychological aspects.
I. Title
QA11.2 .S65 2002
510/.19—dc21 2002024200

ISBN 0-8077-4241-4 (paper)
ISBN 0-8077-4242-2 (cloth)

Printed on acid-free paper
Manufactured in the United States of America

09 08 07 06 05 04 03 02 8 7 6 5 4 3 2 1

Contents

You can't fight it; twice two is four . . . a wall is a wall.

—Fyodor Dostoyevsky, *Notes from the Underground*

Cells divide in order to multiply.

—Introductory biology text

Preface

What makes mathematics possible? What makes mathematics confusing? And why should mathematics make so many people nervous and uncertain? Could something be wrong with the way mathematics is taught and talked about?

These questions have been an extension of my long study of other human intellectual accomplishments: language, reading, writing, thinking, and learning. Here I focus particularly on the way mathematics is talked about, because language is a frequent source of confusion or contention when called on to explain human mental activities.

I'm not suggesting I had everything planned when I began my inquiries more than ten years ago. Back then I had only a passing acquaintance with mathematics, and had considered little about its relationship to other aspects of human thought. I had no plan except to immerse myself whenever possible in books, reflection, and conversations about mathematics. As I did so, I began to understand why people who are accomplished mathematicians find what I now call the world of mathematics so compelling and so beautiful. I also came to understand why many people find getting into mathematics so frustrating; why so often, sooner or later, they run into a glass wall.

Mathematics isn't necessarily complicated or difficult, nor is it something that is accessible only to an intellectual elite. Mathematics should be open to everyone, provided no unnecessary obstacles are encountered.

Solutions to Forgotten Problems

I came to see mathematics as a vast continent, still largely unknown and rich with resources. People have entered this continent at different points at different times, followed different routes, and opened up different areas, but eventually some trails began to predominate and some regions became well mapped. One could chronicle this exploration in terms of what was discovered, the geography of mathematics, and many scholars have done so. Others have documented the histories of some of the major explorers. One could survey the terrain in terms of the resources of mathematics and the uses that have been found for them. Or write guides and instructional books on how newcomers might find their way through mathematical territory and exploit the resources for themselves. And one could write of the kind of problems that people had to solve in order to explore the territory—the highways and bridges they had to construct and the obstacles they had to surmount.

It is the problem-solving approach that I have taken, because I see the development of mathematics as a story of people, learners as well as experts, striving to understand more about numbers, and about how numbers relate to each other and to the physical world (including especially spatial relationships).

Mathematics today includes an immense array of solutions to problems encountered and solved in the past. The solutions themselves may be a source of confusion to newcomers who don't know what the original problems were, making everything seem arbitrary. Instead of trying to understand the basic geography, they have to make sense of infrastructure, the complex systems of roads and bridges that may conceal the actual territory being covered.

The path I have finally taken on my journey to understand what makes mathematics possible, but also what makes it difficult, is as follows:

What in general can be said about the territory we are exploring? (Chapter 1: *What Is Mathematics?*)

What is the equipment—the mental equipment—that all people take to explore new territory? (Chapter 2: *Making Sense*)

Where do numbers come from? (Chapter 3: *The Mathematics in Language*)

Where do numbers go? (Chapter 4: *The Meanings of Numbers*)

Why are numbers the way they are? (Chapter 5: *Numbers (I): The Names;* Chapter 6: *Numbers (II): The Written Form*)

What basic things can be done with numbers? (Chapter 7: *Labeling, Ordering, and Quantifying;* Chapter 8: *Calculating and Measuring*)

How not to get lost. (Chapter 9: *Notation—Signposts in the World of Mathematics*)

Different aspects of numbers. (Chapter 10: *Numbers Between Numbers;* Chapter 11: *Numbers in Space*)

What are the best ways to manage numbers? (Chapter 12: *Memorizing, Calculating, and Looking Up*)

What is the best way to learn? (Chapter 13: *Getting Beyond the Glass Wall*)

Who Is This Book for?

I hope this book will offer insights to readers interested in thinking about mathematics, who would like to know better how to learn mathematics (or teach it), or who might be interested in coming to understand why they find mathematics so difficult to learn (or to teach). The discussion should interest teachers involved in any aspect of primary education, and anyone concerned with mathematics, language, thought, and the *potential* of the human brain (or more precisely, of human beings) in general.

I don't presume in this book to declare how mathematics should be taught, except for constant reiteration that it has to be learned with understanding. There are no testimonials for particular methods or materials, because these don't make the difference in the long run. What makes the difference in learning is *understanding*, not of how mathematics relates to the physical world, but of the kinds of relationship that exist within mathematics itself. What makes the difference in teaching is insight into what each individual student might find interesting and comprehensible, rather than frustrating and difficult. Teaching and learning depend on shared understanding, which is not something instructional methods and materials can generate or curriculum guides ordain.

You don't have to be a mathematician to read this book. With a few gentle exceptions, there are no graphs, equations, formulae, exotic symbols, or complex calculations. I examine aspects of language and mathematics for readers who may not be linguists or mathematicians themselves.

Thank You

to Mary-Theresa Smith, as always, for outstanding editing and constructive suggestions;

to Karl Nyberg, my production editor, for doing so much to make the text coherent, especially the fractions, mathematical notations, and diagrams;

to Bryant Fillion, Constance Kamii, Stephen Krashen, and Judith Newman, for years of friendly support and good advice;

to innumerable authors who have helped me think about the topics in this book, often before I knew I was writing it.

Introduction

Let me summarize at the beginning what I examine in detail in the remainder of this book. I am going to talk about two different worlds, the *physical world* and the *world of mathematics*, and about the *glass wall* that exists between them.

The physical world is our familiar world of objects and events, directly accessible to our eyes, ears, and other senses. We all have a language for finding our way around the physical world, and for making statements about it. This everyday language is often called *natural*, not because other kinds of language are unnatural, but because it is the language we all grow up speaking, provided we have the opportunity to hear it spoken by family and friends during our childhood.

I use the word "world" metaphorically to talk about mathematics because it is a completely different domain of experience from the physical world. (I used a different metaphor in the Preface when I referred to mathematics as a continent, still largely unknown.) Mathematics can be considered a world because it has a landscape that can be explored, where discoveries can be made and useful resources extracted. It can arouse all kinds of familiar emotions. But it is not part of the familiar physical world, and it requires different kinds of maps, different concepts, and a different language. The world of mathematics doesn't arise from the physical world (I argue)—except to the extent that it has its roots in the human brain, and it can't be made part of the physical world. The two worlds are always at arm's length from each other, no matter how hard we try to bring them together or take for granted their interrelatedness.

The language used to talk about the world of mathematics is not the same as the language we use for talking about the physical world. But problems arise because the language of mathematics often looks and sounds the same as natural language. The same words and phrases may be used in both languages, but they have different meanings, depending on whether they are used to describe aspects of the physical world or aspects of the world of mathematics. This can be a source of great confusion. "Five is a prime number" is a statement in mathematical language. "Here are some ripe bananas" is a statement in natural language. "Here are five bananas" is a statement that mixes natural language with mathematical language. "Five" may look like natural everyday language, but its meaning lies in the world of mathematics, not in the world of physical objects.

Finally, the glass wall is a barrier that separates the physical world and its natural language from the world of mathematics. The barrier exists only in our mind—but it can be impenetrable nonetheless. We encounter the wall whenever we try to understand mathematics through the physical world and its language. We get behind the wall whenever we venture *with understanding* into the world of mathematics. At any time, from the very beginning of an acquaintance with mathematics, we can find ourselves stymied by the glass wall, on the outside looking in.

Those are my major points. The rest is elaboration.

A Question of Language

We'll see in this book how major problems can arise when mathematics is approached as if it were part of natural language. Trying to talk one's way through mathematics can make it baffling. And to find oneself lost in incomprehensible surroundings is aversive; it can create phobias.

Mathematics is not a language, at least not the kind of language that linguists study. It has a different kind of grammar and vocabulary from natural languages, at least one of which we learn to speak with relative fluency in the first few years of life. Mathematics doesn't translate directly into any natural language. If we want to call mathematics a language—because we can use it to communicate ideas—then we are using the word "language" metaphorically.

Our physical environment and mathematics are worlds apart. There is nothing remarkable about this. Music is yet another kind of world. It has its own landscapes to be explored, its own grammar and vocabulary, and it can't be translated into natural language—or into mathematics, for that matter—even though it can generate similar kinds of emotion.

To understand and appreciate music, you have to get inside music. To understand and appreciate mathematics, you have to get inside mathematics. Everyday language is of limited help in getting into the heart of music or mathematics, and can arouse confusion and frustration.

The Authority of Numbers

Mathematics often has an authority that makes it look as if it is part of the physical world. When someone tells us there are four eggs in a basket, we can see four eggs in a basket, seemingly in the same way that we can see brown eggs, or small eggs. But how do human beings make sense of number? Numerosity is not a physical property of eggs, like color or size. Where do we get the idea of number from, if not from language?

Most discussions of mathematics, even those concerned with teaching basic arithmetic to beginners, take numbers for granted. Children are "taught" to count, in the sense of reciting a short sequence of number words in the right order and also in the sense of applying those words appropriately to collections of real objects. Children also are "taught" a few simple ways in which numbers relate to each other—that two times three equals six, for example. These mathematical "facts" are discussed discursively in words, often accompanied by "concrete" examples, like two groups of three objects. But none of this makes sense if the listener is unable to understand what the number words refer to. This underlying understanding is never explained.

In this book I examine how numbers become meaningful in the first place, and why some people can soar from their earliest understanding of numbers to the highest reaches of abstract mathematical thought, while others find it difficult to progress beyond their first unsteady mathematical steps.[1]

My particular concern is with how natural language and mathematics are related. (Henceforth I shall just say "language" when I am referring to natural, everyday language. When I am referring to the language of mathematics, I shall say so.) Are they part of the same mental enterprise, or are they different, in the way that language and mathematics are separated as subjects in the classroom and as topics on library shelves? Do language and mathematics spring from the same roots? Do children learn to talk and to do mathematics in the same way? And when mathematics and language part company—how does this happen?

Almost everyone learns to talk, in a very selective way. There are over 10,000 different languages in the world, and almost everyone learns to speak and understand one of them at least. This is a considerable intellectual accomplishment. Why is it that mathematics sometimes can prove such an obstacle for people who have mastered the intricacies of speech, and of reading and writing as well, much of it highly abstract?

The Deceptiveness of the Obvious

One of my aims is to investigate aspects of mathematics that are taken for granted, that might appear "obvious" or "common sense." How do we achieve such certainty? And what was our point of view before something became obvious to us?

Here's a simple example that I return to in detail later:

The meaning of the number "three" (or 3) often is explained by holding up three pencils and saying, "This is what three means," or "This is three." That's obvious; it's common sense. The mathematical concept is explained by the language and the demonstration.

But in fact, holding up three objects to illustrate the meaning of the word *three* explains nothing at all—unless you already know what "three" means. To someone unfamiliar with the concept of three, who hasn't learned what numbers mean, the statement, "Here are three pencils," assumes what it is supposed to illustrate. Why should someone unfamiliar with numbers think that quantity is what the three pencils are supposed to represent (as opposed to being made of wood, writing instruments, yellow in color, or an assertive gesture)? The "explanation" is like showing a pencil to a color-blind person to illustrate what the words "yellow" or "color" mean.[2]

Here's another example. What's the opposite of "more"? Common sense tells *us* the answer is "less." But that particular example of common sense is something we have acquired in the context of mathematics. To a child at home, the opposite of "more" is usually "no more," or "nothing."[3] Parents who refuse a child who asks for more of something don't usually take away part of what the child already has. Teachers who try to tell a child that the opposite of more is less may run into a blank stare.

For as long as we regard something as obvious, we overlook the intelligence that went into making it self-evident. It took the human race many centuries to establish a conceptual system so that it is possible to understand what is meant when a person refers to "three pencils," or "less than three." Human infants usually achieve such insights relatively quickly, but not because the insights are common sense. The insights still represent giant steps for the human mind.

The Glass Wall

While some parts of mathematics may seem obvious, other parts, to many people, are dauntingly obscure.

At some point, for many people (not excluding the author), mathematics changes from something that is comfortably self-evident to something else that is dense and impenetrable. The transition is often abrupt. We may glide through a textbook as easily as a bird flies around in open space—and suddenly we collide with a glass wall. We can't understand the nature of the obstacle because we can't get to the other side. All we know is that we have gone as far as we can go, for the moment at least. We might try to slog our way around the impediment with determination and rote memorization, but we don't know where we are or how we can travel further. Our minds are stuck in the physical world.

Mathematics, Inside and Outside the Head

Mathematics can be found in two locations. A small part is firmly situated in our head (or in everyday language) and a vastly larger part constitutes a world of its own.

The part of mathematics that is in our head, whether we are children at the threshold of learning about mathematics or the most accomplished professional mathematicians, is very limited indeed. It comprises a few basic concepts that are already established in spoken language, a rudimentary contrast of numbers (basically one and more than one), and a very general sense of quantity (like being able to *see* that three objects are different from two objects, without the need or ability to *count* the number of objects). This may not seem very much, but it is the basis of all the mathematical knowledge that has ever been discovered and all the mathematical techniques that have ever been invented.

The rest of mathematics is accessible to our understanding only to the extent that we venture into its domain. The endless succession of numbers available to us is essentially incomprehensible outside mathematics, and so are all the mathematical procedures that can be undertaken with them. We may learn how to use such numbers, and to engage in calculations and other operations with them, often to great personal advantage and even enlightenment. We may remember multitudes of mathematical facts. But to understand them through everyday language is beyond our capacity. Mathematics can only be understood mathematically.

There is nothing unusual about this constraint. There are all kinds of things that we become familiar with, respond to intellectually and emotionally, and can predict and even exploit, that are "out there," part of a world outside our head. Like the planets, the weather, and the oceans. Like music. Like human fabrications such as architecture, automobiles, and computers. If we want to find out more about them, we have to look outward, into the objects themselves, not into our own mind. We can think about them, but they are always separate from us.

Natural language is not like that. Language has a particularly intimate relationship to the human mind. The meanings that we attach to words and statements come from inside us; they are attached directly to thoughts existing or immanent in our mind, and to the emotions behind them. Not only can we understand language, but the language in our mind is the basis of most of our understanding of the physical world and of our relationships with everyone and everything else in it.[4]

But this language is not capable of providing an understanding of mathematics, except to a very limited extent—again, only as "one" and "more than one," and only in a rough-and-ready way. The huge mass of mathematics, except for the tiny fragment that is language-based, is inaccessible except through the world of mathematics. We can think about the rest of mathematics, but only through thought about mathematics.

It is a complex and unfamiliar idea, and a radical one, that only a very small part of mathematics can be put into everyday language. The idea is developed throughout the rest of this book.

CHAPTER 1

What Is Mathematics?

Someone is bound to ask what *exactly* I'm talking about when I use the word "mathematics," and I must answer that I can't exactly say. This isn't sloppiness on my part, I hope, but a reflection of the fact that natural language and the language of mathematics are fundamentally different.

Semantic issues inevitably arise with natural language. The language of mathematics is never ambiguous, and there is never any doubt about what a mathematical statement means.[1] The word "mathematics" is not a mathematical term, but a part of natural language. When I say that it is impossible to understand mathematics through the medium of natural language (as opposed to the language of mathematics), that is not because there is something peculiar about mathematics. Ambiguity and imprecision are inevitable in natural language,[2] and are the reason that mathematics, music, computers, card games, and knitting patterns have to have special languages; they cannot tolerate the ambiguity of everyday speech.

Ask mathematicians what mathematics is,[3] and you'll get a variety of answers. You may be told that mathematics is the science of numbers, or the study of patterns, or a language, a form of logic, an art, a system of symbols and rules, a tool, even a mental discipline. All of these responses are valid as partial descriptions. They are metaphorical means of looking at mathematics (like my referring to mathematics as a world). But they don't explain what mathematics is. None of the statements sums up what might be called the essence of mathematics, certainly not in a way that would be informative to anyone who had never had the opportunity to encounter mathematics; to a child, for example. In other words, language doesn't tell us much about mathematics as a whole, any more than it does about music.

Dictionaries don't help. Dictionaries offer descriptions and examples of how words are used, but not insights into what words refer to (see Note 4, Introduction). They don't even guarantee the existence of whatever a word refers to. My dictionary describes imaginary creatures. It also defines truth, beauty, justice, and morality, which also aren't things whose essences you can inspect personally, or get people to agree about. No one can appeal to a dictionary for authority on theoretical or philosophical issues.

The definition of mathematics in my dictionary alludes to an "abstract science of quantity" that embraces three more specific "sciences"—geometry (concerned with the "measurement of space"), arithmetic (concerned with numbers and reckoning),[4] and algebra (concerning relationships among symbols). All of this may be true, as far as it goes, but it doesn't go very far. Geometry, arithmetic, and algebra aren't exclusive or comprehensive domains of thought or activity; they overlap, and leave out other significant areas of mathematics. Besides, mathematics is surely more than a science or collection of sciences. It is something that most people do, and know something about, even if they aren't scientists and wouldn't claim to be mathematicians.

The philosopher-mathematician Bertrand Russell had a short answer to the question of what mathematics is: it is what mathematicians do. But once again, people who aren't mathematicians do mathematics. If you can talk, you can hardly avoid mathematics. Mathematics isn't so much a particular way of behaving as a large number of particular kinds of activity (just as writing may be composing a poem with a ballpoint pen or completing a tax return on a computer).

Obviously, one enormous aspect of mathematics involves numbers, the focus of this book. The essence of this aspect of mathematics lies not so much in what you can do with numbers as in the relationships among them—what it is about 1, 2, 3 and all the other numbers that makes them work so productively together in calculations, with a precision and reliability unique in human experience.

There are other aspects of mathematics that don't involve numbers at all. Some aspects involve spatial relationships (concerning, for example, shape, speed, and direction, or surfaces and holes). Many people find it useful to think about numbers in spatial terms. Other aspects involve logical relationships (for example, that if A is greater than B, and B is greater than C, then A must be greater than C). Numbers themselves can be analyzed in terms of logical relationships without precise calculation.

It shouldn't be surprising that neither mathematicians nor dictionaries seem able to define what the essence of mathematics might be. "Mathematics" is a word; that is all. And like most words, it can be used in a multitude of ways. We can examine some of the things that are done in the name of mathematics, and reflect upon what might make these things possible, but struggling to define exactly what constitutes mathematics won't get us anywhere.

The Meanings of "Mathematics"

The word *mathematics* has multiple meanings. For a start, it may refer to what people *do* or to what they *know*. Many people engage in activities of a mathematical nature without being aware that they are doing so, for example, when they take it for granted that spending some of their money will leave them with less, or that the weight on one side of a balance has a relationship to the weight on the other side. *They do without knowing.* On the other hand, many of us can recite mathematical knowledge that we never put to use, concerning perhaps the celebrated square on the hypotenuse or the identity of a few prime numbers or square roots. These are facts embedded in memory rather than skills expressed in behavior, like the dates of ancient battles once learned by rote. *We know without doing.*

Some people, obviously, know many more facts of a mathematical nature than other people, though probably no two individuals have exactly the same collection. Probably no two individuals have exactly the same repertoire of skills either. And there is far more to mathematics than any one individual could actually know or do. I doubt if all the people in the world together know all the mathematics in all the mathematics books, journals, and Internet sites that exist today.

No one could say that the mathematics that exists in books and other archival sources exhausts all the mathematics there ever will be. The evidence is the reverse. Professional publications on mathematical topics proliferate, on paper and in electronic form. No one can read fast enough to keep up with everything being published on mathematical topics. In fact, the more mathematical knowledge that is developed, the more relative ignorance there must be.

There are, then, four general ways in which the word mathematics is used:

1. "Mathematics" may refer to knowledge that individuals possess of a mathematical nature, concerning, for example, addition and multiplication tables; the nature of odd, even, and prime numbers; percentages; exponents; roots; and quadratic equations. Some facts that individuals possess may not be found in mathematics texts; they do not have formal status. Mathematics in the "knowledge" sense may be far removed from a science; it is a collection of things that individuals know (or believe).
2. "Mathematics" also may refer to skills that people exercise in certain kinds of circumstances. Different individuals may have quite different repertoires of skills, which also may differ from procedures formally set out in mathematics textbooks, just as the way individuals actually talk and write may be quite different from examples set out in grammar books. Mathematics in this "operational" sense is again by no means a science; it is a variety of things that people do.
3. "Mathematics" may refer to everything that has ever been expressed on a mathematical topic. This is literally a "world of mathematics" since it exists independently of individuals, and would exist in books and other

memory devices, available to be decoded and rediscovered perhaps by visitors from another planet if no humans were left on earth.

4. "Mathematics" may refer to potential realms of knowledge and power stretching beyond any point that human venturers have so far reached, but which nevertheless may be entered and explored.

Everyone can be mathematical, even without knowledge or understanding of mathematical formulations that are laid out in texts and expounded in classrooms. Everyone is sensitive to the "one thing after another" that is the basis of numerical mathematics. We can assess, compare, contrast, and calculate (though we might not use a conventional numbering system); we can recognize similarities and differences.

Many people calculate their change—and even figure complex profit and loss balances and interest margins—according to systems they have devised themselves, even though they could not understand the identical but abstracted concepts in textbooks.[5] Mathematics is not something imposed on people or inserted into them; it comes *from* them. The mathematics in textbooks is not a description of the way people actually think and do mathematics. Perhaps a few new terms are required for "doing mathematics," "being mathematical," or "understanding mathematics," to distinguish the act from the abstraction (as we have distinctive terms for the acts of "speaking" and "writing" to distinguish them from the abstractions of "language" and "grammar").

What Is Mathematics Like?

Mathematics is like many other things in some ways, but not exactly the same as any of them.

Despite frequent analogies, mathematics is not a language in the way speech is a language (though like art and music it may be a means of communication). Most of mathematics is certainly not like a "natural language" that infants in every culture rapidly learn from the people around them, nor is it a "foreign language" the way Lithuanian, Japanese, or English might be for speakers of other languages. Natural languages are intertranslatable—anything said in German, or Swahili, or even in a dead language like Latin or Sanskrit, can be translated into any other language (with a little contrivance for specialized vocabulary). Some mathematical statements can be put into speech, though often with a great deal of circumlocution and loss of precision, but it is impossible to go the other way. Try putting the language of a poem, or of a movie review, into mathematical form.

Mathematics has only a skeletal grammar and vocabulary. It is primarily a large number of relational facts (which once may have been worked out systematically but now must usually be taken at face value). Knowledge of mathematics is more like knowledge of geography than like knowledge of language—and like knowledge of geography it depends to a large extent on the particular journeys an individual has made. "Mathematics-talk" is used and understood primarily by mathematicians. Expert mathematicians usually teach only graduate students, who already have a good idea of mathematics-talk, the way committed computer users understand "cybertalk." The more abstruse mathematics becomes, the fewer people mathematicians can talk to professionally, even among their own colleagues.

Mathematics is also not like music, though music-like harmonies may be found in mathematics and both can be said to be founded on "patterns." Mathematics isn't constructed from notes, chords, harmonies, rhythms, and tempi the way music is. A symphony can't be experienced in the form of a mathematical equation or diagram.

Mathematics could be regarded as a story, except that it has no characters and a complex and constantly unwinding plot.[6] The analogy is approximate, but helpful. Like mathematics, stories must be internally consistent and logical—even if the topic is chaotic.

Stories are the way we make sense of experience. We impose stories on the world and construct worlds with our stories. Anything we can't make a story of, we can't understand. Events and relationships in stories may not always reflect events and relationships in the physical world. But within the story, there has to be consistency and therefore there is the possibility of truth. Characters exist in stories, and what happens to them in the story is real (in the terms of the story). Does Hamlet exist? In the play, yes. Do ghosts exist? In the play, yes. When Polonius is pierced by a sword, he conforms to imperatives of the dramatic world in which he exists—he bleeds and dies.

Do numbers exist? In the world or story of mathematics they do, whenever they are used or thought about. They behave according to the imperatives of the mathematical world. What about the infinity of numbers that have never been used or even thought about? They also exist—potentially. It is the same with any human construction.

Do buildings exist? Of course. Where? In the physical world. Where does *knowledge* about buildings exist? To some extent in people's minds, but mainly in books and in the structures of buildings that already exist. Do buildings exist before they are built? Potentially—an infinite number of them. Where? Nowhere; not yet. Things with potential existence don't have actual existence, and don't reside anywhere.

After all the negatives, can anything positive be said about the nature of mathematics? In a very general way, mathematics (like language, music, architecture, art, sport, and courtly love) is attributable solely to the creative way human beings are capable of thinking. We wouldn't have mathematics if we weren't capable of thinking in mathematical ways. Mathematics, as an enterprise, is a product of human imagination and creativity, involving curiosity, contrivance, discovery, reasoning, learning, understanding, interest, and effort.[7]

Mathematics is also a social phenomenon, involving not only the way other people perceive us and deal with us, but also the way we perceive ourselves in relation to other people. Finally, it is an interactive activity. People develop mathematics by engaging their brains with mathematics that already exists, in a variety of forms. All mathematics, even the most original, depends on the mathematics that has been done before. How mathematical we are depends to some extent on our personal histories. And like everything else that happens to us, mathematics also involves luck, or chance, in the way our personal histories have unfolded.

Mathematics sometimes may be congruent with the physical world, but only to the extent that we select and organize aspects of that world to suit our mathematics. It is a match rather than a reflection. Mathematics may fit very neatly for simple calculations in carefully circumscribed situations. But complex phenomena, like physics, economics, and psychology, need a lot of modeling and curve-fitting to make mathematics roughly applicable. People asking whether the world is mathematical should explain exactly what aspects of the world they are talking about.

Even so, the match between mathematics and physical reality is sometimes remarkable. The dimensions and weights of physical objects respect our mathematical laws, even if we submerge them in water or hurl them through the air. Sunrise and sunset conform to the mathematical constraints we place on them. Over 100 years ago, mathematicians correctly calculated the existence of planets hitherto unknown and unsuspected. The universe seems to follow our mathematical laws—a fact capitalized upon by cosmologists who use mathematics—and nothing else—to test their theories of how the universe itself began.

In the long run, the physical world and the world of mathematics have to be in concordance with each other because it is not possible for us to live in two different kinds of reality. It shouldn't be surprising that all the mental constructs we lay upon the world, like the evidence of our different senses, fit together into one coherent consistent whole, about which we all agree. If this weren't the case, the world wouldn't be what it is, and we wouldn't be who we are.

Inevitable and Invariable

Mathematics reflects its own logical and computational relationships, not anything about the way the physical world (including the human brain) is put together. The world of mathematics could exist if the human race became extinct; even if there were no physical world as we know it. The structures of mathematics do not need a human brain or a physical world to support them. By definition, two plus two would equal four in any universe. By definition, squares and circles would have the same geometrical properties in any universe in which squares and circles could exist, or be imagined. All mathematics requires in order to persist is somewhere to be made manifest. And for centuries that place has been the most flimsy of footholds—small pieces of paper.

From the time that our forebears ceased writing on rock to the time when texts and data began to be stored electronically, there was one predominant place where mathematics existed, and that was on paper. There has always been some mathematics—relatively little—in human minds, but the enduring bulk of it was and still is on paper. That is the reason there has long been more mathematics around than any individual or group of individuals could be acquainted with; no one could possibly read it all, let alone understand it all. It is the reason that mathematics could survive even if human beings left the scene—because it could persist on paper, or in electromagnetic fields, until some other intelligence came along to interpret and develop it. It is also the reason that mathematics could, in principle, outlast the end of our world—voyaging timelessly in spacecraft or as packages of radio waves (like the communications routinely sent to space probes).

Our creations become the environment in which we live. We have the illusion that we are in charge of our creations because we constantly tinker with them and "use" them, but they change us as much as we change them. We no longer invent the worlds in which we live, nor do we deliberately make them what they are. We have to explore these worlds if we want to see what they have become, and sometimes to see what we have become.[8]

The Origin of Mathematics

There are many speculations about "how mathematics began." A popular scenario envisions a shepherd putting pebbles in his pockets to ensure that the same number of sheep came back at night as went out in the morning. But this superficial view doesn't account for the insight that went into mathematics, not into the relationship between pebbles and sheep but into the relationship between pebbles and numbers, or between numbers and sheep, and into the all-important relationships among numbers themselves—the very idea of number. The edifice of mathematics demands rather more substantial foundations than worry about whether all the sheep are accounted for. It requires imaginative minds.

The realization that there are more, less, or the same number of pebbles on one occasion compared with another depends on an existing mathematical understanding. And in any case, how could the genius of one apocryphal shepherd disseminate itself over large parts of the globe? It wasn't an individual who gave birth to mathematics; it was the human race.[9]

Two things must have gone into the mix from which mathematics sprang. One is the general development of the human brain, when it reached a degree of complexity and imaginative power—when *homo* became *sapiens*—almost certainly related to consciousness and self-reflection. There is more about this in the next chapter. And the other is a fertile social and cultural environment.

What made mathematics take off so spectacularly, from a small and rudimentary counting system to an enormously complex and never completed mass of knowledge, was—mathematics itself. The moment mathematics stopped being simply something that people did in their heads, intuitively and informally, and became a system that was represented in written form, it became public property, to be examined, reflected upon, and expanded. It wasn't in the human brain that mathematics developed, but in the interaction of the brain and mathematics itself.

Mathematics in its written form probably preceded and may well have engendered written language. And both written mathematics and written language probably derived from drawing, or the graphic representation of events (or rather, ideas of events), on sand, rock, and later paper. Back in this undifferentiated past, mathematics would have had the same roots as language, art, maps, diagrams, and other forms of expression.

While the basic concepts of number, measurement, and fundamental calculation were universal, because they derived directly from human language and thought, technologies of mathematics—like notational systems and conventions for representing numbers—varied widely. They were no longer ways of thinking but means of doing.

Discovery or Invention?

Is mathematics discovered or invented? This final question, again, is not easily answered, not because of any essential mystery in mathematics, but because of the imprecision of language. At one point the difference between the two terms might have seemed obvious—something is invented if it did not previously exist, and something is discovered if it previously existed but was unknown. Manufactured devices and processes are invented, and the properties and possibilities of natural phenomena like air, oil, crystal, or rubber are discovered. But once someone has invented and created an artifact, it achieves the status of a natural phenomenon—other people may discover or rediscover it. And discovery itself may be self-initiated and directed, so that it becomes a kind of invention.

One would think that language is something that is discovered by every child (or taught to every child). Yet studies of the rapidly efficient manner in which language skill and knowledge develop in children has led many researchers to assert that language is invented (or reinvented) by children rather than discovered by them or revealed to them. And no less a psychologist than Jean Piaget has asserted that children have to invent or reinvent mathematics in order to learn it.[10] In a sense, the wheel is reinvented every time someone discovers what a wheel can do.

Other aspects of mathematics (and language), both historically and individually, are the result less of discovery or invention than of the exercise of imaginative reason. This sometimes is referred to as *conceptualization*, or *insight*, but it might just as well be called "good ideas." It is the sudden realization of how things go together, how they are internally structured or externally related. It is "seeing" how things fit together, for example, in a jigsaw puzzle or a chess problem, in the construction of a piece of furniture or a piece of computer programming.

Knowledge is constantly being created—sometimes in the duplication of what someone else already knows, sometimes in the rediscovery of what was once known but subsequently lost, and sometimes in genuinely original new invention. The scope and scale of mathematics are vast. Nevertheless it is all, actual and potential, invented and discovered, consensual and idiosyncratic, the product of one thing alone—the human brain, interacting with a world around it; in this case, the world of mathematics. The route we shall take to try to get an understanding of mathematics begins by reflecting upon the nature of the brain itself.

CHAPTER 2

Making Sense

Before surveying how people might make sense of mathematics, we should consider how we make sense of anything. What is it about the way we think that makes mathematics (and language, and everything else) possible? And what is it about the way we think that erects barriers to our own intellectual development?

People are imaginative, curious, and inventive. We learn many things without effort (sometimes things we might be better off not learning); other things we have difficulty learning and remembering no matter how hard we try. We hate restrictions and limitations, dislike incompetence (including our own), and abhor boredom. We are emotional, and have feelings. We can learn, often quite unnecessarily, that there are things we can't learn, and we can learn, also quite unnecessarily, that we are inadequate in various ways. We can learn the wrong way to learn something. All this is relevant to mathematics.

I know some readers will object to the previous paragraph, on behalf of others and possibly themselves. They will say there are people who have very little emotional range, whether for joy or sadness, that many people can't learn, lack imagination, relish incompetence, and even tolerate boredom. This may be so—though always to a degree and usually as a consequence of experience. I don't propose to debate any of this here.[1] Instead, I want to outline systematically some major aspects of human thought and predispositions, particularly conspicuous during childhood, that are most relevant to an understanding of how mathematics could develop at all.

Four Unique Characteristics of Human Brains

Four unique and universal characteristics of human brains make mathematics and all other human accomplishments possible (and even, I would argue, inevitable):

1. What human beings *seek* in the world in which they find themselves
2. What they *expect* from that world
3. What they *bring* to that world
4. How they *respond* to that world

The presence of these characteristics needs no explanation or justification; it is the way people are. Without these characteristics we would live in a different kind of world—or rather, the world and people as we know them wouldn't exist at all.

The world to which I refer at the moment is the physical world, but the four characteristics apply equally to the world of mathematics and to any other world we might experience.

1. People *seek* organization and structure in their experience, they seek relationships and interconnections. They look for *sense* in the world, by which I mean they don't expect things to be random or arbitrary. They also search for utility and relevance to themselves, for ways of achieving ends. In short, they look for ways in which the world is predictable and for ways in which they are part of the world.[2]
2. People *expect* to find three things in the world, which might be referred to as the "three Cs." They expect consistency, coherence, and consensus. By *consistency*, I mean we all expect the world to be the same tomorrow as it was today and yesterday. I'm not saying that there won't be change or unexpected events, but that these themselves will occur in consistent ways. The world isn't wayward. It behaves predictably, even if we often don't know enough before particular events to predict exactly what will happen.[3] By *coherence*, I mean that we expect to find everything hanging together. We don't expect bits of the world, or of our experience, to be unrelated to other bits. And finally, by *consensus*, I mean that we expect other people to view the world and their experiences the same way we do. I don't mean that we expect everyone to have the same opinions or beliefs, because obviously we don't. But we do believe and expect that the world we live in is the same for everyone—that the rain that falls on me falls on the person next to me, and that the sun we see setting in the evening is also setting for our neighbors.
3. People *bring* to the world an ability and pervading propensity to categorize all the objects and events in their experience, and to look for (or establish) multiple relationships among these objects and events.[4] From these categories and relationships, people form generalizations and abstractions that enable them to capitalize on their experience and broaden their understanding of the world. I also should say that people bring language to the

world, although language, like mathematics, is a product of all the factors I am considering. The language we use summarizes and determines the way we view the world. And finally, people bring a sense of story to the world, which might be termed a sense of how things should fit together over time. We make sense of our experience in stories. We communicate with each other in stories. And we look for stories, not just in language, but in actions, images, sounds—and numbers.

4. People are *responsive* to the world; never detached from it. Everything we do affects the world around us, and everything taking place in the world around us affects us. In effect, individuals (or their brains) and the world around them (including other people) constitute an integrated system. No man is an island. This interaction of brain and environment is not just an empty truism. Our intimate and inescapable relationship with the wider world in which we live is the basis of all our thought, action, and learning.[5]

What Is a "World"?

I use the term "world" in the very broadest sense, to refer to everything outside an individual that is capable of influencing and affecting that individual's behavior and thought. We can start with the "natural world," the environment that existed before the hand of human beings was laid upon it. I refer here to the world of land, sea, and sky; night and day; weather, rocks, and trees; and living creatures of all kinds. Many of these are accessible to our senses—the sights, sounds, textures, smells, and tastes of which we are aware.

But I'm also including the multiplicity of things that human beings have put into the environment, so that much of the original "natural" world is often concealed from us. I call this enhanced environment the "physical world." It includes every technology, from roads and buildings to ships and aircraft, and computers. I also include all the maps and diagrams, symbols and notational systems, that enable us to navigate our way through the world, both natural and fabricated. I don't distinguish the fabricated part of our environment from the natural world—in fact, I'm sure that infants and every other living creature regard human artifacts simply as parts of the world in general. We have to learn to categorize what is "natural" from what humanity has furnished.

This extended "world" of objects and persons is more than just a physical fact to which we have to accommodate. For a start, the world is an enormous memory resource. There is far more knowledge in the world than there is in anyone's head, perhaps more than there is in *everyone's* head, and I'm not referring just to books.

The dials and levers and switches in a car remind us of how to drive a car. (They would be evidence to an extraterrestrial about ourselves and our way of life.) Maps and signposts remind us of the route we want to take, and the road itself guides us to where we should place our vehicles and the path we should follow. The keyboard of a computer reminds us of how we should operate our fingers to achieve certain effects, the handles on doors remind us how to open doors, and cutlery and crockery remind us how food should be consumed. The fact that we normally take for granted all of the myriad things we routinely find in the world doesn't mean they play no part in our behavior. To a large extent they control our behavior.

And they take a load off our mind. Everything our environment reminds us of is something our brain doesn't have to store in detail. Our intentions, like our feelings, may have their origins in our head, but the manner in which we carry out a large part of our activities is supported if not controlled by situations and structures outside ourselves.

I distinguish mathematics as a different world because we cannot get access to it through the senses (except in a superficial sense), or through language. Mathematics is entered, explored, and utilized only through *reason.* Like the physical world, it contains its own structures, but the structures in this case are strictly mathematical. Like music, it is a unique and independent world.

We sometimes think these external structures must be in our head because, for example, we can imagine driving a car without actually getting into one. But what we have done is internalize the car. First we interact with a "real" car in the world outside our head, then in effect we put the car into our head and drive it in our imagination.

The same reciprocity occurs with mathematics. We employ pencils and paper to do calculations that might be impossible in our head alone. But with experience, we can *imagine* doing these calculations. We put the pencil and paper back into our head. We do the same with speech, constantly, when we rehearse something we want to say to someone, or simply "talk to ourselves." We can never escape exterior worlds, not even in our fantasies.

What Brains (or People) Do

The intellectual capacity of homo sapiens should never be underestimated, even when we look and feel like bewildered bunglers. We are highly complex and competent. We constantly create and explore new worlds, logical, functional, actual, and imaginary. We do this—initially—solely with the equipment with which we are born. But almost immediately we recruit other people and employ what we find around us to increase our knowledge and develop our powers.

I have mentioned our constant propensity to put things into categories, to establish relationships among those categories, and to give those categories and relationships names. All this gives us an immense intellectual handle on the world. Without categories, we would be unable to differentiate anything. The world would be either one vast pudding-like whole or an infinite disorder of unconnected ingredients. Without relationships among categories, nothing would be related to anything else and our mind would be full of meaningless rubble. And without names, there would be no way of thinking about anything, let alone talking about it.

We are born with a host of predisposed ways of organizing experience into which mathematics smoothly fits. We have an innate sense of time's arrow, so that we expect one thing to follow another. Our sense of structure is like a yardstick that we lay over events, or a thread on which experiences can be strung. We don't view life as a jumble of unrelated occurrences. Instead we have a profound feeling for *sequence*, for cause and effect, for intentions and outcomes, and for things having an appropriate place in the temporal fabric of our lives.

We have a similar innate sense of the spatial extension of the world, and of the fact that we can move around in this world of space. We can observe everything in the world—including ourselves—from different points of view. Because we can see how people and objects relate to each other, and to ourselves, in time and space, we can *triangulate* (a mathematical term adopted by theorists to describe how people locate objects or even ideas in the world). We can see the same world with and without our presence (the view of a god, or of the impersonal omniscient narrator of a saga). And all of these things that we can do literally we can do metaphorically, through language and imagination. We can think.

We are born with the basic ideas of arithmetic—with notions of one, some, more, fewer, the same, and "not the same." We are sensitive to size, volume, weight, movement, and relative speed. We are born with the basic ideas of geometry—of space, shape, position, direction, distance, area, boundaries, and straight lines. And we are born with the basic ideas of algebra—that one thing can stand for another, and that what applies on one occasion can apply in similar circumstances on other occasions—the great human powers of abstraction and generalization.

We pursue ideas beyond immediate relevance or utility, and thereby venture into many areas of theory, including "pure" science, "pure" mathematics, and art. Numbers fall comfortably into our images of time and space, though we may not feel so at ease with numbers when we encounter them on their home ground, the world of mathematics, displaced from our familiar world.

We are born with powerful abilities to recognize patterns, as we do when we distinguish faces, places, and spoken and written words. We recognize sequences and similarities, as we do with music. We are able to complete patterns when we see only a part of them, when we get a glimpse of a face, hear a fragment of a melody, or detect the aroma of coffee. And we are able to impose patterns on configurations that might otherwise appear to be randomly formed, like the figures we find among constellations of stars or the images we see among flickering dots of light on television screens and computer monitors. We can make patterns, innumerable hosts of them, among the numbers and other structures of mathematics.

Since we are so adept with patterns, it might reasonably be asked what a pattern is. A pattern is anything in which we can find a predictable sequence. Patterns don't exist in any world; they exist in our head. We know when we identify, find, or complete a pattern because we have a feeling of satisfaction, a sense of closure. We have found what we sought.

This agreeable feeling of closure is part of what I regard as a uniquely human characteristic—a *sense of good fit,* or *sense of appropriateness.* This sense isn't much talked about, but it is crucial to the way we make sense of anything. It tells us when we can stop puzzling, when we have found a solution. An example is finding the right piece for a hole in a jigsaw puzzle, when we say, "Aha," and can move on. Otherwise we want to try again—or to give up. Our sense of good fit leads to conventions, which make possible much of mental life and all of social life. We have conventions for everything—including appropriate ways to be unconventional.

It is because life so often obliges us by conforming to our expectations that we are able to capitalize upon our innate tendency to abstract and generalize. We don't regard the world as chaotic. Rather we expect that everything will submit to our reason and conform to the way we expect things to hang together. Our sensitivity to order and our preference for predictability don't necessarily always work to our advantage, and we often display a limited tolerance for uncertainty and ambiguity.

Add a few more ingredients and you almost have a human being: language, reflection, imagination, curiosity, inventiveness, mimicry, and a readiness to explore and exploit the natural world, until we learn caution and restraint. What is left? Emotions, the gamut from hope to fear, love to hate, joy to despair. Our inmost feelings about ourselves and the world are the driving and directing force behind all our learning, understanding, and creativity.

No image of a person would be complete without the shading of unproductive characteristics. We get confused and discouraged, construct negative images of ourselves, become antagonistic toward others (even when they might be trying to help us), and give and get the wrong messages. We are human; we are fallible. All this must have played a part in the development of mathematics, and it certainly plays a part when we try to become mathematical ourselves.

Going to the Limits

To summarize this chapter: Human beings have a creative brain that we use to make sense of our experience. With our knowledge and technologies we construct worlds that become potent in their reciprocal effects on human beings, as prompts, memory, and guides. An intelligent mind and a fertile environment together constitute a powerful creative force, and complex systems are bound to develop.

From this it follows that all of our technology is inevitable. Humans were bound, sooner or later, to develop ways of extending their thinking power, just as they were bound, sooner or later, to magnify their strength, amplify their perceptual abilities, and increase the speed at which they traveled across the earth, and explored and exploited the seas, the skies, and even outer space. Every small step humans took to augment their powers became a rung on a ladder that they could climb to increase their abilities and their ambitions. But there is never any climbing down (unless hostile forces attempt to destroy our knowledge or technology for us). Humanity (as a whole), harnessed to its developing technological and intellectual accomplishments, always pushes on to the limits.

Like most human technology (and institutions), mathematics is a *feed-forward* system. The more you have, the more you get. *Feedback* systems tend to support steady states and constant control. Feedback from the thermostat on a heating system keeps the temperature steady. If the temperature goes down, the furnace switches on; if the temperature goes up, the furnace switches off. But with a feed-forward system, any move away from the steady state is magnified. Whatever is being generated is amplified until it goes off the scale, or exhausts itself.

Mathematics didn't reach a dead end when computers were developed. Instead, computers have allowed mathematics to flourish to the point where it is sometimes out of sight for human intelligence. Where mathematics will lead us is literally incalculable.

CHAPTER 3

The Mathematics in Language

Mathematics has never been entirely independent of natural language. Its beginning must have been in general concepts that were already available in spoken language, such as *one, next,* and *more.* And many mathematical ideas continue to find expression in everyday language, for example, numerical order and ideas of profit and loss. But the understanding that makes these spoken words meaningful in a mathematical sense still has to come from mathematics.

Mathematics must have its roots in *spoken* language, but there is no evidence of how this happened, only conjecture. There are many relics of the struggle to put mathematics into a *written* form, from which it eventually could develop profusely; it is a story of continual trial and error.

We could surmise that attempts to put both language and mathematics into visual form had a common origin in the representations of objects and events, loosely referred to as "cave art," as early as 40,000 B.C.[1] Archeological discoveries suggest that written forms of language and mathematics developed at roughly the same time, between 3000 and 2000 B.C., in areas of the world as diverse as Egypt, Persia, India, and China. Before that time, "spoken mathematics" must have been an indistinguishable part of spoken language, with a limited set of numbers, or rather quantities, and a few rudimentary ways of counting, measuring, and calculating. But by 2200 B.C. mathematical tables were in existence, and mathematics was widely used for trade, legal, and scientific purposes (as well as for taxing and for lending money at interest).

The development of written forms of both natural language and mathematics was never easy. People strove for hundreds of years to find the most practical way of making language visible, beginning with "picture writing," arbitrary signs, phonetic symbolism (like using a pictorial symbol of a sun for words with different meanings that sounded like "sun"), syllabic writing systems, and finally the alphabetic principle that seems to be in the process of taking over the world's writing systems.[2]

For mathematics, the main problems were to find ways to express numbers economically, without having to think of a unique name and shape for every number, and to set out numbers in a visible form that was both compact and efficient for calculation purposes. As with the alphabet, there is a long history of different cultures struggling to achieve solutions in their own way (while borrowing parts of solutions from neighbors). But while thousands of cultures developed different forms of spoken and written language, they all were concerned with what are essentially the same set of meanings, or concepts. And the variety of solutions that were devised for problems in representing numbers and their relationships were all concerned with essentially the same underlying structure of numbers.

In the previous chapter I outlined some of the innate conceptual structures that make mathematics (and all of our rational lives) possible. Now I look at some of the *words* that reflect these inborn concepts, forming an essential part of the way we think and talk. These words stand outside the gates of mathematics. We all think and talk mathematically, long before we learn any mathematics. Mathematics and natural language are not distinct ways of thinking; they are simply different domains of experience to which human thought can direct itself. Language and mathematics do not demand separate and unique mental faculties, even in children.

In the Beginning, the Words

Mathematical concepts are conspicuous among the first words that children say and understand, reflecting mathematical structures in the underlying thought that shapes and drives language development.

We could begin with some of the most forceful words that every infant utters: the primal, "I want one," followed by Oliver Twist's immortal, "I want *more*."

"One," "the," "a," "this," and "that" demonstrate concepts of *identity* and *categorization*, as do "same," "different," and "another." "These" and "those" demonstrate *plurality*; "none" and "nothing" demonstrate the other extreme.

"Want one," "want some," "want another," "want more," "want it all" similarly demonstrate a nonnumerical understanding of *quantity*, while the notion of "shares"—frequently expressed by children as "not fair"—reveals a grasp of *proportion* and *ratio*.

The understanding that "yesterday" is past and "tomorrow" still to come demonstrates a sense of *sequence*, as do "now," "when," "then," "next," and "my turn."

"Here," "near," "far," and "now," "soon," and "a long time" demonstrate relative *distance* in space and time; "big" and "small" demonstrate relative *size*; and "fast" and "slow" demonstrate relative *speed*.[3]

Geometrical concepts are revealed in such early vocabulary as "straight," "crooked," "round," "pointed," "begin," and "end," as well as in "here" and "there," "up" and "down," "long" and "short," "above" and "below," "thick" and "thin," and "side," "inside," and "outside." The geometrical and mathematical concept of *change* is ubiquitous in language from its earliest stages.

Universals of Mathematical Language

The number system is fundamentally a matter of one thing after another, of "more," "again," or "next," of progression and succession. These are the threads with which we weave all our perceptions of the world, and talk about them. The order in which familiar events occur can't be rearranged without disrupting the narrative line of our explanations and expectations, the webbing that holds all our experience together.

Every language distinguishes singular from plural. The number distinction is conspicuously marked in grammar and vocabulary, as fundamental as the temporal distinctions of past, present, and future, and the gender distinctions of masculine and feminine. Plural forms of nouns, verbs, and other parts of speech differ from singular forms—he *walks*, they *walk*. Plural forms are frequently irregular—one *child*, two or more *children*—an indication of their long and independent history in the language. Number (but not numerals) is fundamental to the way we see the world, and talk about it.

The primal concept of more is augmented by terms like "add," "increase," and "expand," and contrasts with terms like "reduce," "remove," and "diminish." Notions of replication and multiplication contrast with dividing and distributing.

Mathematics thrives in a small but fertile field of language. Anyone who can talk has the essential mental competence to engage in mathematics. The structures that generate understanding of language and mathematics are the basic ways in which the mind works, aspects of the meaningful frames the brain lays over the chaos of uninterpreted experience.

Perception, Language, and Mathematics

We perceive people and objects as individual entities, as units, which we put into a multitude of categories constructed through language. We also distinguish people in complementary (or oppositional) forms, as male–female, tall–short, liberal–conservative, friendly–unfriendly, and so forth. We distinguish other creatures as cats, dogs, cows, and sheep, and we distinguish objects as planes, trains, trees, and rocks. This immense but organized complexity is possible only because we can think in terms of individuals, collections of individuals, and equivalences or differences—the membership of *sets*.

Behind many of our categorical distinctions, and perhaps the basis of them all, is inclusion–exclusion. Either you're a child or not a child, a Canadian or not a Canadian, a mathematician or not a mathematician. This is *binary* thinking, the basis of digital electronic technology, perhaps the most elemental and powerful means of mathematical computation,[4] though historically not the first.

Some substances merge with themselves so easily that it is difficult to grant them individual identities, as particles of air, water, flour, or salt. And because we can't make them singular, we can't pluralize them and talk about "two waters," "three flours," or "four salts." They can't be counted. With no convenient singular or plural forms, we have to put such substances into a special category of "mass nouns," which often create awkwardness in language. When mass nouns refer to collections of people, as they occasionally do, like crowds, governments, and committees, we are never quite sure whether to say "it is" or "they are," to treat them as singularities or pluralities.

Mass nouns also create complications in applied mathematics. Where we can't count we have to measure, which means that new concepts have to be constructed. In place of "two waters," "three flours," or "four salts," we have to measure and calculate in terms of volumes of water and weights of flour or salt.

The categories and relationships that we see in the world do not originate in the world; they originate in the brain, and continue to exist only there. That is one reason why mathematics can never be explained by pointing to examples in the world—"Here are *three* pencils"—unless the appropriate mathematical concept (of "threeness") already exists. It is also the reason why people who *can* see mathematical relationships are nevertheless always anxious to point to examples in the world for the illumination of those who can't—"Can't you *see* I've got three pencils?" They feel that what *they* see is obvious, not realizing that the basis of their conviction of threeness is in their own mind, not in the pencils they are holding.[5]

When we perceive two or more objects or individuals in the world, we often notice that one is taller, or larger, heavier, older, paler, hairier, happier, or wiser, or has more of any other of a multitude of possible attributes. We make comparisons. Once again, there is nothing of these comparative relationships that is inherent in the world. There is nothing about a tree that makes it "taller" than another—we impose the relationship ourselves.

And without ever receiving formal instruction, we can make logical deductions about comparative relationships. We know that if Ann is taller than Ben, and that Ben is taller than Carol, then Ann must be taller than Carol.[6]

It is not necessary to cite comparatives like taller or bigger to exemplify the contrastive relationships that exist in the brain but not in nature. Simple attributes like tallness and bigness are themselves relative—to whatever else is regarded as a standard or a yardstick. The most common basis for comparison is the human body. Anything bigger than we are, is "big."[7]

Rhythm and Rhyme in Human Knowledge

The human brain has entry into many different worlds, or domains of experience. One of the most obvious is the world of music. Music in its own right appeals profoundly to all our emotions, with the power to seize our mind and our muscles, setting us off on trains of thought or of rhythmic movement. And musical rhythms provide sturdy hooks from which memories can hang.

Poetry and song are obvious examples of the way in which the rhythms that are so often a conspicuous part of music can be found in conjunction with words. At a more elemental level, rhythmic chants pervade children's play and adult thought, far more perhaps than we generally suspect. Chants are a fundamental element in language, language-based knowledge, and mathematics.

Much of our learning is in the form of lists or sequences, many learned as chants, like the days of the week and the months of the year. Familiar chants like:

Sunday, Monday, Tuesday, Wednesday, Thursday, Friday, Saturday

or

January, February, March, April . . .

and so forth are much easier to recite, and even to read, than unfamiliar sequences such as the alphabetically ordered:

Friday, Monday, Saturday, Sunday, Thursday, Tuesday, Wednesday

or

April, August, December, February . . .

Differences in the ease of reading or reciting these unfamiliar sequences have nothing to do with the order in which the days and months actually occur, but derive from the fact that we have learned the original sequence almost like a song, as an unbroken melodious string, which can be repeated only in the way in which we originally rehearsed it.

Indeed, if we want to know the day that comes three days after Wednesday, we probably have to use our fingers and work our way through the week, just as most of us have to recite, "Thirty days hath September . . ." to work out the number of days in the current month. Much of our systematized knowledge is in the form of simple rhymes and chants.

Mathematical Chants

The fundamental mathematical chant—the basis of our earliest numerical experience—is what mathematicians call the natural numbers (or sometimes, informally, the counting numbers). I refer to it as the "number chant":

one, two, three, four, five; six, seven, eight, nine, ten

(The semicolon indicates the conventional point at which to pause for breath or break the rhythm.)

Sometimes the number chant takes a more poetic tone, as with the sequences that begin "one, two, buckle my shoe . . . ," or "one–two–three–four–five, I caught a fish alive. . . ."

I spelled out the numbers one to ten rather than put them into their arithmetical form:

1, 2, 3, 4, 5, 6, 7, 8, 9, 10

because the numbers are first learned as words, not as a part of mathematics. Mathematical convention subsequently eliminates the 10 from the written sequence (because it is double-digit) and adds 0 (zero) to the beginning, creating what mathematicians sometimes call the number line:

0, 1, 2, 3, 4, 5, 6, 7, 8, 9

which is not a chant in anyone's language. And no one counting a collection of objects, even in pretence or play, would begin with "none."[8]

These inconsistencies are the first of many important differences between spoken and written aspects of mathematics. The number chant itself turns out to be a handicap if it is too deeply embedded in our mathematical thought; it is only one of an infinite number of possible ways of organizing numbers, and deserves no special priority.[9]

Children usually learn the rhythm of the number chant before they learn the order of the number words, and long before they know what the number words mean and how they can be used. But they recognize—or take it for granted—that order is important. If they recite the chant in an idiosyncratic order, they will tend to repeat it in the same order (just as they will repeat incorrect versions of songs that they have only partially learned or understood). Children demonstrate their understanding of the importance of order in the act of counting before they are sure of the conventional order of numbers, so they will consistently "count" with appropriate words in an inappropriate order—one, two, three, five, four, nine, seven. Or they will introduce nonsense sounds to fill the blanks in their knowledge.

Everything in this chapter so far demonstrates children's innate sensitivity to sequence, consistency and order, central elements in mathematics, richly exhibited long before children have learned any formal mathematics. But the richness and sensitivity is still protomathematical—one thing is needed to complete the whole panoply of mathematics, and that is an understanding of *numbers.* Language, as a system, has *number*—the difference between singular and plural—but not *numbers*, the meaning of all the potential relationships among numbers. Children may be able to recite in order the numbers from 1 to 10, and even be able to parrot that the difference between 7 and 4 is 3. But without the comprehension of *why* the difference between 7 and 4 is 3, and *has* to be 3, children are still in the realm of everyday language, not in the world of mathematics. They have not penetrated the glass wall.

I refer to recitation of the first ten counting numbers as a "chant" because it is learned primarily for its rhythm, not for its meaning or utility. Chants usually have no meaning (to the learner) beyond their sing-song quality, whether their eventual utility is alphabetical, numerical, or some other mnemonic function like the names and order of days and months. They are learned like nonsense rhymes, like hickory dickory dock, and they stay in our mind in the same way.

But once these chants are securely lodged in our mind, we can refer to them for a multitude of practical purposes, from working out the day of the week to engaging in the most abstract of mathematics.

Other Mathematical Chants

The chanting of the counting numbers is unique, but it is not the only way in which rhythmic language makes mathematics possible. Other chants have considerable mathematical utility, like the addition tables:

> one and one is two, one and two is three, one and three is four . . .

and the multiplication tables:

> one two is two, two twos are four, three twos are six . . .

The "tables chants," as they might be called, are not productive like the alphabet and the counting numbers; they don't generate anything beyond themselves. They are the ordered recitations of facts, mental cribs, that save us the trouble of having to work certain things out. We don't have to calculate the result of adding 2 + 2, or multiplying 3 × 6, because the chants provide the answers.

The tables chants have one thing in common with the number chant—they usually are learned without comprehension of their mathematical implications. Initially they are just meaningless words, because there is no understanding of how the chants relate to each other, or how they can be related to anything else. A child learning the "times tables" is not necessarily learning anything about multiplication.

The Power of the Alphabet

An enormously productive chant that is not mathematical is the alphabet, learned in the form of a song with a distinctive driving rhythm:

A B C D E F G,
H I J K L-M-N-O-P,
Q R S; T U V,
W X Y Z

(The last four letters don't conveniently scan, and have several alternative tunes and rhythms.)

Like many of the songs we learned when young, the order of the alphabet becomes indelibly impressed upon our mind. The chant forms an unbreakable chain. Many adults have to start from the beginning to say which letter comes after K in the alphabet, and it's almost impossible to recite the list backwards unless the reverse order has been learned as another chant, a different tune.

The alphabet is a rich and productive human resource because it can be endlessly rearranged to form an infinite number of easily distinguishable written words in an infinite number of combinations. What the Greek writer Nikos Kazantzakis called the 26 soldiers of the alphabet can march in different formations to bring us every play, poem, and story ever composed—and there is no indication that electronic technology will make them less vital in the future.

But perhaps as significant as literature for human culture has been the order that the alphabet introduced. Letters of the alphabet perform many of the systematic functions of numbers, sometimes in conjunction with numbers, for example in the Dewey decimal scheme for organizing library materials, on automobile license plates, and in some countries in postal area codes.

Without the alphabet there would be far less order and bureaucracy in our lives. Think of all the class lists and voters' rolls, indexes, and directories that depend on alphabetical order—innumerable objects and references strung together on the basis of a childhood chant, and often dominating our lives. Alphabetical order may be losing some of its predominance, but only because computers can make high-speed searches to find items on unordered lists. As computerization proceeds, numerals acquire more importance as identity numbers in profusion are allocated to us and to many of the objects in our lives, sometimes taking priority even over our names.

Confusing Familiarities

Even the simplest of mathematics can become difficult to understand when precise and unambiguous mathematical expressions are "translated" into everyday language. There can be no argument that 6 + 3 = 9, that 6 – 3 = 3, that 6 × 3 = 18, and that 6 ÷ 3 = 2, from a mathematical point of view. The notational links can be given names—such as *plus, minus, multiply, divide,* and *equals,* and there are also many synonyms—such as *add, take away* or *subtract, times,* and *make.* As long as these terms are taken to refer to particular mathematical relationships—as mathematical language—there is no problem. But if the words are expected to *explain* mathematical relationships, there can be considerable confusion, because natural language and the language of mathematics have different meanings.

I should reiterate that the difficulties exist only for learners and others who don't understand what people using these common mathematical terms are talking about. For anyone familiar with the mathematics, who has no trouble with addition, subtraction, multiplication, and division, the casual use of mathematical language appears obvious. Such people often wonder why beginners can have so much trouble. This is a difficulty for me as an author in writing about such matters. Readers long familiar with *plus, minus,* and all the other technical words may find it difficult to see why the ambiguities I talk about create any kind of problem. Surely their meanings are obvious. I can only suggest that such readers try to imagine the problems they would have trying to understand "simple explanations" of recondite matters they know little about, a learned discussion of quantum physics, perhaps, or microbiology, or postmodernism.[10] There they would encounter a glass wall.

We may think we are using clear and familiar language when we ask a child to add a pair of numbers, or to take one away from another, but unless the child already understands what we are saying *mathematically,* the child will not understand what we are talking about. Explaining or illustrating how the words are used in spoken language doesn't explain or illustrate how they are used in mathematics. I'll give a few examples. (The actual mathematical meanings are discussed more fully in Chapter 8.)

- "*Add*" (or "plus"). Supposedly the simplest part of mathematics, adding is by no means an uncomplicated or self-evident state of affairs, as we shall later see. When used mathematically, the word "add" refers to a specific relationship between numbers that is essentially undefined, a direction through mathematical space. No one *explains* what it means to write 2 + 3 = 5, or to say "Two plus three equals five." The statement is produced, sometimes with simple but misleading analogies, in the fond hope that the meaning and the reasoning will become apparent. And this doesn't always happen. Learners get to feel that mathematical facts like 2 + 3 = 5 make sense because they can be related to some limited situations in the physical world, rather than to quite a different range of situations in the world of mathematics.

When the word "add" is used in everyday contexts, it has quite different meanings. If a recipe tells us to add milk to cake mix, it refers to a physical operation, not a mathematical one. You don't add 2 to 3 the way you add milk to cake mix, water to cement, or love to a relationship. Pie plus ice cream is not the same as 2 + 3.

Two and three don't "make" five, certainly not in the way that soil and water make mud, an athlete makes the team, or an assignment makes the grade. Two "plus" three has nothing in common with a hamburger plus fries, nor is it analogous to the way a hem is added to a garment or a postscript added to a piece of correspondence.

Unless you already understand the numbers two, three, and five mathematically, being shown pencils and being told they are two, three, or five is meaningless. "Two" is not the same kind of word as "yellow," "pointed," or "writing implement."

• "*Minus*," (or "subtract," "take away"). Minus is not a common word in everyday language, and when it is used—"Unfortunately I'm minus my umbrella today," "I was hoping for at least an A minus on the test"—it doesn't have anything like the mathematical meaning.

Terms like "difference" and "take away" are used frequently, but with a sense that has nothing in common with the mathematical relationship of subtraction. The difference between 5 and 2 is not the same as the difference between baseball and football, or between apples and oranges, and 2 taken away from 5 is not the same as a toy taken away from a child or a snack taken away from a fast-food restaurant. You don't take two from five the way you take a glass from the shelf or a candy from a packet. When you subtract two from five, you don't take anything away.

The word "subtract" is rarely used in everyday language, and never in a way that resembles its mathematical sense. Subtraction may be used to compute the difference between the two dollars I have and the five dollars you have, but no money actually changes hands; there is no taking away.

The "minus" explanation also doesn't help comprehension of "negative" numbers, which have the minus sign placed in front of them. There is no real-world analogy for a negative quantity of anything that doesn't involve mathematical understanding.

The terms "positive" and "negative" themselves don't function in mathematics the way they do in everyday language, for example, with positive and negative remarks. Numbers less than zero aren't negative in the way that an answer, a response, or an attitude is negative. A negative number doesn't mean "No." It is not negative the way an electric wire or power source might be negative (which is also an odd use of the term), nor has it anything in common with the negative of a photograph. The complexities of negative numbers can be explained to novices only in terms of mathematics.

• "*Multiply*," (or "times"). Numbers don't multiply the way weeds or rabbits multiply. Multiplication is not repeated addition, either in mathematics or the world in general, no matter how often mathematics textbooks make the claim. Biology textbooks, on the other hand, attest that cells multiply by dividing.

Children usually are told that "multiply" means "times," and "multiplication tables" are expressed in terms of "times"—"four times three is twelve." In normal language, however, the verb "to multiply" doesn't mean "times." It simply means "increase." The biblical injunction to "go forth and multiply" doesn't mean add yourself to yourself a certain number of times; it means have children. Problems are multiplied when there are more of them, but not as a result of repeated additions. A timekeeper who times a race is measuring, not calculating, and so is the person who says, "I've seen that movie three times already."

• "*Divide*." You don't divide a cake the way you divide five by three. The popular analogy of slicing a pie doesn't demonstrate what happens when a number is divided. In everyday language, division means splitting or sharing, not necessarily in equal portions, or disconnecting a part from a whole. Division is not repeated subtraction, either in mathematics or the world in general, no matter how often mathematics textbooks make the claim.

There's a clue in the fact that dictionaries don't offer explanations for the mathematical use of any of the terms I have just listed. In one popular dictionary, for example, the definitions for the verb "to add" go through the "join," "mix," and "increase" type of definition for everyday language, and then offer the vacuous "to perform mathematical addition" for the mathematical sense.

• "*Equals*." The most difficult symbol of all, equals doesn't mean "the same as," "amounts to," or "the answer is." Two plus three doesn't equal five the way five candy bars equal, or are the same as, another five. In mathematics, a number of different things can be done around the sign for "equals"; for example, anything done to one side must be done to the other, and everything on one side can be replaced by everything on the other. There is nothing similar in the concept of equality in everyday language.

In the world outside mathematics, adults and children don't normally say that two things are equal if they are substitutable for each other; instead they say that things are "the same as," "as much as," "as many as," "as big as," or occasionally "can take the place of." They don't say that a cork is "equal to" a screw top for closing a bottle. Frequently used phrases like "equal rights" and "equality of opportunity" have no mathematical equivalence. So what does it mean to tell a mathematical novice that two plus two equals four (or is "the same as" four, or "makes" four)? The flash of understanding—that both sides of the equation are the same number—can come only from inside mathematics.

Many other mathematical terms are used frequently in everyday language, for example, *total*, *place*, *column*, *solution*, and *answer*,[11] but there is no need to belabor the point. Two other familiar terms—*count* and *number*—are such critical concepts in mathematical language that each will require a substantial part of an entire chapter in this book.

Having discredited all of our everyday ways of talking about basic mathematical concepts, can I offer better alternatives? The answer is "No," because mathematical terms can't be translated into everyday language. The language of mathematics is not the same as natural language. I'm not saying the terminology of mathematics can't be understood, because obviously it can. But the understanding of mathematical terminology has to come from inside mathematics, not from the everyday language we use to talk about it.

CHAPTER 4

The Meanings of Numbers

It is often said that children should develop a number sense. Yet most people manage their mathematical lives without a thought about what such a sense might be. If asked, they would probably say that the meaning of the number 4 is four of something. That's obvious, isn't it? But numbers commonly don't make any sense at all outside mathematics, and it is unclear what a "number sense" might be within mathematics. A person may achieve a general understanding of how numbers behave, or relate to each other, within mathematics, but that is hardly a "sense" in the way in which we can have a sense of smell or a sense of touch. Numbers don't derive their meaning from anything in the physical world, but from something in our mind, and from the world of mathematics that minds have created.[1]

The Meaning of Language

All of this is quite different from the situation with language. We don't often hear pronouncements about how important it is for children to develop a "word sense," to understand that words have meaning, or to "develop good word concepts." It is assumed that infants will understand what language is, which is just as well because how could anyone explain to them that words have meaning, and that the noises that people around them persistently make contain some kind of sense? Infants demonstrate this basic insight in the first few months of their lives.

Infants look for order and sense in their experience, and find it for language in the way speech is organized and used. They find the three *C*s of coherence, consistency, and consensus in the sounds that people utter and in the way they respond when such sounds are reflected back to them. Meaning is taken for granted. Anything that doesn't have meaning, that makes no apparent sense, is ignored. The question of acquiring a "word sense," or of understanding that words have meaning, never arises.

I am not saying that children never lack an understanding of the meaning of *particular* words—of course they do. Even adults occassionally will say, "What does this mean?" for an unfamiliar word they have come across. But statements about the understanding of numbers are not referring to particular number, like 5, 9, or 11. You don't hear people say, "I wonder what *fifteen* means," the way they might ponder, "I wonder what *cynosure* means." Instead, the mathematical pronouncement suggests that learners might lack a *general* understanding of numbers, the way an individual might lack any comprehension of a section of computer code, or a genome sequence.

A major reason for the difference between language and mathematics is the special relationship that people have with language. Language is literally at our nerve endings. The meaning of language is inseparable from the way we perceive objects, categories, and relationships in the world. Babies looking for sense and purpose in the sounds they hear around them bring meaning from their own feelings, from their relationship to other people, and from their experiences in the physical world.

But the world of mathematics is not in the person, nor in the physical world, but in a world of its own. It is in the world of mathematics that the meaning of numbers must be found.

The Meaning of Numbers

There are at least three things wrong with saying that numbers are quantities of objects:

1. The answer begs the question. To say that 4 means four of something is like saying that red means something that is red (or the color red), or that wet means something that is wet. The answer doesn't tell you anything; it is circular—four means four.
2. The answer is incomplete. If a number has to represent a quantity of something, what could the number 742,984,347 mean? I don't know anything of which 742,984,347 exist. Yet 742,984,347 is as good as any other number, and just as meaningful as any other number. I don't have to think of something occurring 742,984,347 times before I can do anything with the number.
3. The answer is wrong. Even if the meaning of 4 were four of something, like a handful of pencils, that's not the meaning of 4 in a general sense. We don't have to refer to four of anything to confirm that $3 \times 4 = 12$. We can *calculate* that 3 times 4 equals 12, and we could do that on the back of the moon with no quantities of anything around. Numbers are separate from quantities. Quantifying is something we do *with* numbers, but it is not the meaning of them.

We have to distinguish the meaning of numbers from their utility. What we do with numbers is one thing—like counting, comparing, and calculating. But what numbers are is another matter. This is like the distinction between the nature of bricks and their uses. Bricks can be used for all kinds of building, and for other purposes too. But that is not what bricks are. Bricks are clay or some other material of a certain size, shape, and consistency. It doesn't matter how you use a brick, or even if you don't use it at all; it remains a brick. What is it about numbers that makes them numbers independently of any use to which they might be put?

The answer is that numbers are *relationships*. Relationships with what? With other numbers. Isn't that circular and completely self-referential? Yes—that characterizes numbers exactly. Numbers don't get their meaning from anything except each other.

(Sometimes numbers don't even relate to each other, for example, when they are used as identifying labels on the shirts of athletes. Such numbers lack mathematical properties. This oddity is considered in the next chapter.)

The *basis* of the number system is very simple, consisting of the two concepts already introduced in the mathematical chants—*one* and *more*. Each number is a magnitude. The rest is all relationships. One is one, two is one more than one, three is one more than two, and four is one more than three. One, two, three, four are simply names we put on concepts that we construct (or that others have constructed before us)—a chain of iterated "ones."

From this point we can elaborate. Four is not only one more than three, it is two more than two. It is also two times two, and one less than five. Six is three times two, half of twelve, the square root of 36, and every other relationship we can think of for six. The number 742,984,347, among other things, is three times 247,661,449.

By now we have crossed the border between language and mathematics, behind the glass wall. We are discussing *numbers*, not words. The moment we start building numbers on numbers and examining their mutual relationships, we have left natural language and entered the world of mathematics.

The most complex human achievements are often built upon the simplest of ideas. The idea of placing one block of stone on top of another is primitive enough, but skyscrapers and bridges have been built from elaborations of that basic principle. What could be more uncomplicated than a wheel, a mark on paper, a flame, or a musical note? Even modern electronic technology, with its vast and labyrinthine elaborations, is compounded on nothing more complicated than the opening and closing of switches in electrical circuits.

Imagine an endless supply of building blocks. With one block you can just look at it. With two you can put one on top of the other. With three you can make a tower, a bridge, or a wall. The more you examine the blocks, the more uses you can find for them and the more elaborate constructions you can create. If other people are doing the same thing, you quickly find the landscape covered with buildings and constructions of all kinds, in endless variety, more than any one person could possibly explore or comprehend, while people continue to find new ways of using blocks. It is the same with numbers.

It is the same with music. You want to see what people can do with the basic building block of a musical sound? Look at all the world's songs and symphonies.

Numbers are a self-contained system. They may be rooted in something existing outside mathematics, namely, the concepts of *one* and *more*, but from then on everything in mathematics comes from within the great superstructure of numbers itself. You can't go outside the system to recruit something else into it, such as a color or a musical tone—or a handful of pencils. Once you have determined the meaning of *one*, and of *one more*, you have determined the entire number system and the whole basis of mathematics. You don't know *everything* about mathematics, of course—you could spend your entire life without accomplishing that. But you have provided yourself with a powerful construction kit and the basic tool for expanding and exploring the different things that can be done with numbers. For a while at least, you are on the other side of the glass wall.

The Precision of Numbers

Mathematical calculation can be very precise. We not only know that 3 is greater than 2, but that the difference is exactly 1. If we apply this reasoning to pencils, or to the number of dollars we pay for a bag of potatoes, we feel we know precisely what we are talking about. But the ability to know precisely what numbers mean outside mathematics runs out very quickly.

It is one thing to grasp the mathematical meaning of statements like, "One million is five hundred times bigger than two thousand." But that is a mathematical statement. What does it mean as a description of a state of affairs in the world in general? Does a million of anything—a million dollars, or a million acres—mean anything except that it is a very large number, much bigger than 2000 dollars or 2000 acres? What does 2000 dollars mean to us, or 2000 acres—or even 20 dollars or 20 acres—except in relation to other numbers? Does either statement have any *sense*, apart from what we can gain from the numbers themselves?

What sense can we make of the statement that there are approximately 52 weeks in a year, or somewhere between 28 and 31 days in a month? What do 28, 31, and 52 *mean*, apart from the fact that they are numbers? Can we shift numbers out of their own self-contained (and therefore circular) world and into the world of language, or the physical world, in a form that we can understand?

The answer to all the questions is that all numbers, apart from a handful at the beginning of the number chant, mean nothing at all, except for their relationships with other numbers. We can't imagine large quantities, not with any precision. We can't imagine a million of anything—a million people, a million pencils, a million dollars—much beyond knowing that it is a lot (in some circumstances). We can't imagine 500 of anything, let alone 2000, so what sense can we make of the statement that a million is five hundred times two thousand? This leads to a strange situation. We can say we know that the statement is correct, but we can't say what it means. Or rather, we understand the statement in a mathematical sense, but not in any other.

What size numbers are meaningful to us? Up to four it may be possible to make sense of numbers, or quantities. Above four, numbers are meaningless, except in terms of other numbers, and except for the very general statements we can make about one number being equal to, bigger than, or a lot bigger than another.[2] Some theorists would argue that four is too generous a figure—that three, perhaps even only two, would be more appropriate.

Where do I get the four from? Four is about the limit to the number of things we can actually quantify at a glance—without counting. We usually have no difficulty saying how many birds there are on a fence, or people in a discussion group, if there are two or three of them. Four is more difficult, and five is about as far as one can go without counting. After that, it is *estimating* (like estimating the size of a crowd)—a very imprecise procedure, even among individuals experienced in doing it. Sometimes we may be right if we glance around a room and think we see six people. But often we will be wrong. (And we'll sometimes be wrong if we think there are only four or five, indicating that those numbers are guesses rather than exact perceptions.)

The Number Span

There is a technical name for the ability we all have to identify at a glance how many objects there are in a small group. It is called *subitizing*, or "seeing" how many objects there are without counting; without using mathematics, in other words. The first experimental studies were done in the late 1800s to determine the size of what was called "the number span" (or "span of apprehension"). The answer was seven at the most, and never consistently.[3]

How many black dots are there in the following line?

● ● ● ● ● ● ● ●

Can you say without counting? Try glancing at a handful of coins, or a pile of books. Up to a total of seven, you occasionally may get the correct total from a glance (combined with a good guess). To make certain, you'll have to count. You'll have entered the world of mathematics.

People may be wrong with four or five objects—but not very often—and they may be correct with as many as fifteen—but again not very often. And then only because they are guessing, or trying to calculate in some other way. It could be argued that people who are not in a position to count start guessing after three or four—and the probability of a correct answer depends on how many alternatives there are. Given very few alternatives—four or five—a guess will be right most of the time. Given a lot of alternatives—ten or more—the guess will be wrong most of the time.

Experience helps, but only to cheat the system. It is an advantage if you can give yourself a mind-set to look for pairs or triplets (triangles). And it helps, of course, if the objects are organized in some easily recognizable way, for example into three- or four-cornered shapes. A correct result is then more a matter of calculation, sneaked in before or after the glance, rather than of perception.

Researchers can always tell if people in a subitizing experiment are counting—they require progressively more time to say whether they are seeing four, five, six, or seven objects. Another venerable experimental discovery was that the time required to say how many objects there are in a group stays constant up to about six or seven, after which it starts to grow rapidly, indicating that counting is involved for larger groups. But the result applies only to counting. For *estimating*—looking at a handful of objects and predicting how many there are—it takes no longer for 200 than for ten.

So what is the connection between the number span—a visual limitation—and the meaning of numbers? What we can't see at a glance, we can't visualize, or imagine. Numbers greater than six or seven are difficult for us to comprehend—especially numbers very much greater—because we can't imagine quantities of that size. We can visualize five cars in a parking lot, but not fifty, or 500, except as a mass. Even the difference between a mass of fifty and a mass of 500 is not easily imagined, except that we *know* that one is substantially larger than the other.

We can *relate* a particular number of dollars to something practical, for example, the kind of car we might like to buy one day or the number of days we might spend on vacation. But what we are doing here is reducing something mathematical to something verbal, to a statement rather than a numerical expression. To say that a certain sum of money is enough to buy 1000 automobiles, rather than 900 or 1100, is largely meaningless (except perhaps to a large company thinking of buying a fleet of automobiles—and even then the meaning is "enough," "not enough," or "too much").

This is the reason words like *day, week*, and *month* are so useful. It is easier to think of five days than 120 hours, to think of five weeks rather than 35 days, and to think of four years rather than 48 months or 208 weeks. Even the passage of time is more comfortably thought about in terms of compact meaningful words rather than in unworldly numbers.[4]

The Meaninglessness of Large Numbers

I'm not saying that large numbers aren't meaningful—but that apart from basic distinctions like "more" or "less," their only meaning is within the mathematical system itself. And I have spent some time making this point because it sometimes is argued that people have an inadequate sense of number, or that they lack important "numeracy skills," because they don't "really" comprehend the difference between, say, a billion and a million—that they have the same reaction whether a politician informs them that a particular project will cost five million or five billion dollars.

I think this is true—but I don't believe that mathematical ignorance is the cause or that mathematical training is the solution. Numbers like five million and five billion *are* incomprehensible. As magnitudes they are incomprehensible. They are literally unimaginable. Apart from the fact that five billion is a lot more than five million, there is not a lot to be said about them outside mathematics—that five billion is a thousand times greater than five million.[5] And not only is five million just as unimaginable as five billion, so also is a thousand.

It might seem to help if we divide large numbers into smaller quantities. If we take 250,000,000 to be the approximate number of people in the United States, then a billion-dollar budget item would be the equivalent of $4 for every man, woman, and child in the country. An idea of the size of a slice of the cake may be useful, but it doesn't tell us much about the size of the cake as a whole, especially when there are 250,000,000 slices.

This doesn't mean that people can't *try* to communicate the magnitude of large numbers better, or to understand them. The way to do this is through analogies. To say that five billion is a whale compared with a tuna of five million is a reasonably graphic metaphor (provided one isn't picky enough to ask if it is the length, volume, or weight of the whale and tuna that are being contrasted). If the ocean liner Queen Mary, moored in Long Beach, California, was stood on end, it would be as tall as the Empire State Building in New York. But what does the height of the Empire State Building mean to us, mathematically speaking? Such analogies are popular in everyday astronomy—if the earth were a basketball in New York City, the moon would be a baseball three miles away, and the sun a dome the size of an apartment house on the other side of Washington, DC. These homely analogies don't help us to understand large numbers; they enable us to avoid them, to stay comfortably on the physical world side of the glass wall.

From "one" and "more"—with the precision of "exactly one more"—the entire system of numbers can be constructed, infinite in an infinity of ways, a world of its own. This could not be done without human creativity. Technologies are required—a technology for economically naming endless sequences of numbers, a technology for making them visible in systematic and productive ways, and technologies for performing all kinds of operations upon and with numbers.

The human brain established the first critical relationships of "one" and "more," but then numbers themselves began to impose their demands so that people were prompted to create the inevitable technologies, devising ways of creating and exploring all the relationships within the number system, and of exploiting them for useful purposes. Mathematics and people serve each other.

CHAPTER 5

Numbers (I): The Names

The verb "to count" has two distinct but equally significant meanings in the English language. One sense of to count means *to recite*—to recapitulate aloud the familiar chant of numbers:

one, two, three, four, five, six, seven, eight, nine, ten

I have called this a chant because children often become acquainted with numbers as an incantation with no obvious utility (as learning to recite the alphabet is meaningless to a child with no understanding of reading and writing). Children who can count in the chanting sense are acquainted with the names of numbers, and with their order, but not necessarily with their uses. But what they demonstrate about order is important. The invariant order is essential to mathematics, though for children it is simply the way they learn any song or chant. They know you don't mess around with the words. It is no more "right" to say "one, three, two," than it would be to say "a, c, b" or "hickory dock dickory."

The simple chant that children first learn to recite, and that everyone takes for granted, is the beginning of the solution to a problem that plagued our ancestors for millennia—to find a convenient and efficient way of finding names for numbers.

The other major sense of the verb to count is *to tally* or quantify, to use numbers to determine the total of something. This is the meaning of the word when we talk about counting our change or the number of birds on a fence. Counting in this sense is a mathematical act, which I consider in detail in Chapter 7. It is the counting system itself that is the topic of the present chapter.

Computation Without Numbers

In the beginning—according to mathematical mythology—there was tallying without numbers, thought about totals before the development of counting. Such tallying is an aspect of protomathematics, the grey area between language and mathematics, and a starting point for many children.[1]

The archetypal tallying fable involves a shepherd dropping a pebble into a pouch whenever a sheep is released into the meadow in the morning, and taking a pebble out of the pouch, as each sheep returns to the fold in the evening. If any pebbles remain in the pouch, then some sheep are missing. If no pebbles are left, all sheep are accounted for. And if there are more sheep than pebbles, a stray has wandered into the flock or a mistake has been made.

There is already a considerable intellectual achievement in this first simple activity. Despite the obvious dissimilarity, each pebble is taken to be equivalent in some way to a sheep. Each pebble "stands for" a sheep. It is easier to get pebbles to line up in rows than sheep, and easier to compare heaps of pebbles than heaps of sheep. But it is not mathematics. There are no numbers with which to describe collections of pebbles.

Mathematics arrived with the realization that the *number* (meaning total) of pebbles was equal to the *number* (total) of sheep, an insight that required a counting system be established. The mathematics lies not in the relationship between pebbles and sheep, but in the relationship between pebbles (or sheep, or anything else) and *number.* Many centuries must have passed before the descendants of the apocryphal pebble-shuffling shepherd had a system of numbers that could mediate between heaps of pebbles and flocks of sheep. Or before a system of numbers could be used to get intellectual control of time, space, and innumerable other aspects of human experience.

Many other scenarios have been proposed in which tallying without numbers might have developed apart from shepherds contemplating their flocks, including monarchs reckoning the size of their armies, merchants bartering grain or spices, farmers awaiting a flood or a harvest, and sailors recording the duration of a voyage. It is all fancy, of course. No one really knows.

Tallying probably emerged in different ways in different places at different times, in small steps rather than giant leaps, as logical and inevitable "next steps" in human development that came with social organization, with planned activities like hunting, trade, or war, and with the technologies involved in large-scale building and agricultural projects.

The earliest concrete examples of what might be a tallying system are small pieces of animal bone etched with rough notches or scratches, usually interpreted as hunters' records of their kills. But it is difficult to see the value of such a tally. It would be meaningless to show the bone to someone else and say, "This is how many bison I've slain this season," before there was a concept of number. Nor would hunters have been able to compare the notches on one bone with those on a bone from another person or time, beyond observing that the notches happened to "look" more, less, or the same.

What the shepherd and hunter lacked—and what the tally system itself lacks—is a method of counting. They were a long way from realizing that seven pebbles *as a total* could represent a *total* of seven sheep, because they had no word "seven," and no meaning to attach the word to. There was still no concept of number.

Comparing Tallies

Shepherds probably weren't satisfied to ensure that all their sheep returned to the fold every evening. They must have wanted to compare the size of their flock with that of their neighbors, or with the number of sheep they had at the beginning of the season.

A simple way to make this judgment would be to compare heaps of pebbles, to say, "I've got more pebbles than you, so I've got more sheep than you." If shepherds could compare their pebbles with a flock of sheep, they could compare them with other heaps of pebbles.

Such comparisons would be made on the basis of a familiar visual attribute, the relative size of a heap. Shepherds probably were already making judgments of bigger, smaller, or the same in other circumstances. They would not even be doing anything original if they put the piles or pouches of pebbles into their hands and compared their relative weights. They might even use a term like "more" in a mass sense—as in, "He's got more porridge than me." They were still not operating with a *numerical* concept of more (or less, or the same).

A similar handicap would apply with the next hypothetical technological development, which was for the shepherds to line up their individual collections of pebbles in rows, and to compare the length of the rows. The idea of putting pebbles in a row might have come from the use of tally sticks, similar to the hunter's piece of bone, where objects or events were represented by a line of notches.

Rows of pebbles or of notches may be a useful visual aid for comparing totals, but they still don't constitute a mathematical device. If my line of pebbles is longer than your line, then I may conclude that I have more sheep than you. And I may be wrong. The pebbles must be equally spaced. Extending a line by making pebbles further apart doesn't increase the total of pebbles or sheep. To compare two lines, the individual pebbles in each line must be paired off. What matters is the *number* of pebbles, a mathematical insight.

This is something that children don't instinctively understand. Celebrated demonstrations by the Swiss psychologist Jean Piaget showed that children often believe that four candies widely spaced are "more" than five candies closer together, that

•   •   •   •

is more than

• • • • •

This is not because children "can't count"—you don't need to count to pair off candies—it is because such children haven't achieved a concept of number. They can see "more" in terms of size, but not in terms of quantity. They understand "how much," but not "how many."[2]

From Pebbles to Beads

There is in English and many other languages a permanent memorial to the significant role that pebbles played in the development of mathematics. The Greek word for a small pebble is *calculus.* The word survives, of course, as the name of a sophisticated method of numerical analysis (*calculus*), and as the root of the English word *calculate.*

Pebbles aren't in great use any more as computing devices, but they probably gave rise to the technology of the abacus, which quickly became universal, and remains in wide use today. Instead of being laid out on the ground, small pebbles were placed in grooves in a small slab of stone. The Greek word *abacus* means a slab of stone. The grooves in the stone of the counting device were later replaced by strands of wire, threaded through beads that took the place of pebbles. And once a decision was made about how many beads should be put on each wire, the whole thing was placed inside a small wooden frame that could comfortably be carried around, like a handheld electronic calculator.

Figure 5.1

The abacus and the grooves in sand or stone from which it developed are occasionally referred to as counting frames. But the term is inappropriate. The abacus is rarely used for counting, in the sense of tallying the total of something, though it did contribute crucially to the development of an efficient number system. Far more important in practice, up to the present day, was the function of the abacus as a calculating frame, for manipulating numbers.

A DEVELOPMENTAL HISTORY OF NUMBERS

The word *number* has at least three meanings:

1. It can refer to spoken *words*, as when we say "one, two, three," or "five hundred and seventy six."
2. It can refer to written *numerals*, as when we write 1, 2, 3, or 576.
3. It can refer to an abstract system of *ideas* (or concepts), for example when we think about "3" (as opposed to "three sheep"), "576," or "3 times 192 equals 576."

Devising the spoken words and the written numerals (meanings 1 and 2 above) were distinct technological problems, each requiring an inventive solution. But understanding number as an abstract system (meaning 3) was a profound conceptual problem, requiring new ways of thinking.

The first great conceptualization had to be that there was such a thing as number, that it made sense to think and talk about mathematical quantities rather than physical properties like size, weight, or mass. But how could you think about quantity without a number system? That was a challenge, to say the least. And the answer was: a little bit at a time. The full-blown idea of number did not occur to any one person, or at any one time.

The Birth of Numbers

Spoken language would already have words for "one"—meaning a single object—and for "more than one" (or "many"). In many languages, the indefinite article "a" or "an" is the same as the word for "one," for example, the French *un* (or *une*). And many nonmathematical terms for more than one persist, for example "some," "few," and "several." What mathematics needed was the idea of organizing a series of "more than one" in a systematic manner, and identifying each successive element in the series with a distinctive name.

The crucial first step was to give a distinctive name to "one more than one." The moment one and one were called "two," then two could be thought of as an independent entity. (Languages sometimes recognize two as an independent conceptual unit outside of mathematics—the way English talks of a *pair*, *couple*, or *brace*.)

The idea of a number *system* would then have been consolidated by giving a distinctive name to "one more than two," which of course is called "three."

As numbers were named, statements could be made about them independently of the objects to which they were applied. One more than three became four, and one more than four became five, consistently and unarguably, whether or not sheep were involved. Numbers became things people could talk about.

The world of numbers had been discovered, and mathematics parted company from natural language and the physical world. Anyone who couldn't understand this remained outside, staring at a glass wall.

The Difference Between Size and Order

The first conceptual breakthrough need not have come with numbers used in a counting sense (one, two, three . . .). It also could have come with numbers that indicated order in a sequence (first, second, third . . .). Words for "first" and "next" would have existed in everyday speech. With the mathematical insight, the one next to first became "second," the one next to second became "third," and so on.

Counting numbers technically are referred to as *cardinals*—referring to "size"—and sequential numbers as *ordinals*—related to order. Since the same numbers are used for both cardinal and ordinal purposes in written mathematics, the technical terminology is rarely employed in everyday life, and won't become an important point in this book. But it should be recognized that numbers have these two quite distinct functions, and that a learner's ability to use numbers in one way doesn't entail ability to use them in the other.[3]

In order to count, in the sense of reaching a total, it is necessary to understand both cardinality and ordinality. To count objects, seven stones or seven sheep, each must be counted once and once only, using *numbers* in their correct order—one, two, three . . . meaning first, second, third . . . (the *ordinal* use of numbers)—with the final number used (seven, in this case) being recognized as the total, the *cardinal* sense of the word.

There is a universal tendency to assume—often fallaciously—that if a word exists, then what it refers to must have existence. For example, if it is possible to refer to a just person, or a happy one, or an intelligent one, then some thing called justice, happiness, or intelligence also must exist, the "true" nature of which can be determined by inquiry, reflection, or argument. The impulse to "reify"—to regard abstractions as realities—has persisted through the ages in many fruitless philosophical and doctrinal controversies—and continues today.

An inclination to regard the first and second pebbles in a groove (or sheep in a field) as having the property of "oneness" and "twoness," or of "firstness" and "secondness," would help give rise to the idea that numbers have an independent existence, waiting to be named and put to use, without necessarily being attached to particular objects or relationships in the physical world. Numbers could be examined as objects in their own right, and useful or remarkable discoveries could be made about them. Philosophy has made an enormous conundrum out of all this, with endless debate over whether numbers constitute a reality of their own, independently of any mathematical function. But inconclusive philosophical debates have not inhibited the prolific elaboration of the number system itself.

Wanted: Names for Numbers

The idea of giving names to numbers was a necessary first step in the advance toward a coherent mathematics, but two technical developments were required before mathematics could become both precise and manageable. Numbers—in the abstract—are endless, and so are potential *names* and *shapes* for them, but human memory has its limitations. The required developments were:

1. a systematic way of identifying numbers so that new names need not be endlessly devised and remembered. (Imagine having to remember a unique and special name for every number we might encounter, just as all the individual people we know have their own names.)
2. an efficient written form for numbers so that numerical situations could be recorded and communicated, and so that extended operations could be performed on numbers, making calculation possible.

Naming was a problem for speech, and representation a problem for writing. We assume that the way we say numbers—"sixteen," "fifty nine," "a hundred and seven"—is fully reflected in how they are written—16, 59, 107. But spoken and written numbers are relatively distinct systems, as we shall see in the following chapter.

SOLUTIONS AT THE FINGERTIPS

The need in spoken language was to find a succession of names for "one," "one more than one," "one more than one and one," "one more than one and one and one," and so on, in a form that was easy to understand, manipulate, and remember.

The first technology of counting was literally close at hand. It was the arithmetical utility of fingers. Tallying probably was done with fingers long before sticks and pebbles were employed. Children frequently move into counting and calculation through the use of fingers, and the word we often use for individual numbers—digits—relates counting to fingers. Fingers were the original digital computers, and the original names of numbers were body parts.

The idea of counting, and of communicating about quantities, through the use of various body parts seems universal. Sometimes the range extends across one hand, sometimes across two, with or without the inclusion of the thumbs. Many groups of people didn't stop there, but continued on with their toes as well and even with wrists, elbows, shoulders, knees, and other body parts. They were carried away by the idea that numbers could be indicated by parts of their body.

Fingers could have provided inspiration for naming different numbers, depending on which fingers were employed. They also could demonstrate how the naming of numbers, or the numbering of objects, should proceed sequentially, in an order as fixed as the progression of fingers on the hand. The names of the relevant body parts would be recited systematically, in a ritualistic fashion—the origin of the number chant.

The Base System

The fingers and hands method was the basis for the next conceptual leap—that numbers could be put into groups that themselves could be individually named and counted. Instead of "five fingers," you can say "one hand." Instead of having to devise and remember a unique name for twenty-five, you could refer to five fives, or five hands, or a handful of hands. Referring to five fingers as "one hand" and ten fingers as "two hands" must have been the precursor of the technology of grouping numbers into tens, hundreds, thousands, and so forth, a profound inspiration that made possible both the expression of infinitely large numbers and the productivity and convenience of mathematical calculation.

Grouping numbers in this hierarchical way is referred to as a *base system*, and the size of the group is referred to as the base. Our conventional method of counting by successive groups of tens is a "base-10" system.

Instead of the memory and representational problems of finding unique names for every number (and running out of body parts), it became possible to use a basic set of numbers over and over again. In a base-5 (one-handed) system, seventeen is three hands and two fingers. You could count to twenty five—a handful of hands—or even to a hundred and twenty five—a handful of handfuls of hands—without having to memorize more than five names (for one, two, three, and four fingers, and one hand).

Of course, you could go much further with handfuls of handfuls, but then the memory and complexity problems arise again. The alternative—and this was another technological breakthrough that took many cultures many centuries to adopt or achieve—was to employ a full two-hand count of ten as the base, and then to give distinct names to groups, and groups of groups, as well.

Thus the numbers up to ten were individually named as the units (one, two, three . . . up to nine). The groups of ten were given distinctive names (ten, twenty, thirty . . . up to ninety) derived from the unit numbers (ten, two tens, three tens . . . nine tens), after which another distinctive name was coined for a group of ten tens—a hundred. The names for the hundreds were then constructed directly from the units (one hundred, two hundred, . . . nine hundred) up to the next plateau of a thousand. No new words are required for tens or hundreds of thousands, but then we have millions, and beyond that billions, trillions, and even more astronomical numbers that few of us need to be familiar with. This is the *decimal* system (from the Greek word for ten) in which numbers are ranked in successive groups of ten.

Grouping also solved the problem of how many beads to put on each wire of the abacus. As many beads would be put on each wire as there are units in the base system. For a base-10 system, each bead on a second wire could represent an entire length of ten beads on the first wire. And each bead on each successive wire could represent an entire length of ten beads on the preceding wire.[4]

Grouping numbers on the basis of tens, tens of tens, tens of tens of tens, and so forth, introduced another vitally important element into mathematics, namely, order in the component parts of number names. When expressing a number bigger than nine, the larger components come first (just as the arm comes before the hand, and the hand before the fingers). We say "six hundred and sixty six," not "sixty six and six hundred," or "six, sixty, and six hundred." There are a few conspicuous exceptions in many numbering systems, like "seventeen" instead of "ten-seven" in English, or "four twenties" (quatre-vingts) instead of "eighty" in French, and also in poetic or colloquial use—like the five and twenty blackbirds of the nursery rhyme. But the general principle of largest-element-first is predominant when talking about numbers, and invariant in written mathematics. It makes possible the systematic organization of numbers on paper, and all numerical calculation.

The actual names given to the different numbers or groups of numbers are arbitrary, of course, and in different languages may be allocated in an idiosyncratic way as a result of historical chance. The English system has "eleven" and "twelve" where consistency might suggest "one-teen" and "two-teen." French, after behaving fairly systematically through the tens as far as sixty ("soixante") suddenly surprises with sixty-ten ("soixante dix") for seventy. None of these oddities is reflected in the written forms of numbers.

Despite the occasional inconsistency in naming, the economy and productivity of the base-10 system are enormous, for both spoken and written mathematics. With barely 25 distinct names—nine for the numbers "one" to "nine," perhaps half a dozen novelties between "ten" and "nineteen," eight more for groups of ten from "twenty" to "ninety," plus the words for hundreds, thousands, and millions—billions of different numbers can be expressed.

And they can be expressed systematically. Once you know that nine follows eight, you know that four hundred and nine follows four hundred and eight, and that nine hundred and twelve is greater than eight hundred and eighty six. Even large numbers are easily placed in order. As a means of establishing sequential order, and of arranging or identifying numbers on sight—the base system is unparalleled.

Alternative Base Systems

The base-10 system is not the only or necessarily the best basis for the construction of a numerical system. Popular alternatives have been 12 and 60, and important systems employing these bases are still in use today.

The division of the year into 12 months of approximately 30 days each was a decision based on astronomical considerations. It is the amount of time, roughly, the earth takes to complete a circuit around the sun (or *vice versa*, as originally was thought) and the moon to complete a circuit around the earth. The decision to subdivide the day into 24 hours, the hour into 60 minutes, and the minutes into 60 seconds was an arbitrary choice of base-12 and base-60 systems. "Angular measurement," by which a circle is broken down into 360 equal pie-shaped parts, or degrees, also reflects the base-60 system, with each degree divided into 60 minutes and each minute into 60 seconds. There is nothing necessary about the particular choice of any of these units. The military uses a "mil" system to divide circles of fire into 6400 parts, rather than the 360-degree system.[5]

One system today challenges the preeminence of the base-10 system. The binary (base-2) system employed universally in "digital" computers and other electronic devices has only two numbers, zero and one. As soon as you count past one, you have to go back to zero again—one, two, three, four, five, six are 1, 10, 11, 100, 101, and 110, respectively. The binary system has some very special advantages that make it useful for computer functioning and computer arithmetic. In effect, each 0 and 1 can represent the closing and opening of an electronic gate or switch.

There are a couple of reasons why the binary system is unlikely ever to be employed for human mathematics. The first is that binary numbers very quickly become space-consuming—75 in the decimal system has to be written 1001011 in binary—and the second is that binary numbers quickly become impossible to say and to remember—there are no special names for numbers beyond zero and one. Neither of these is a problem for computers, which have large memories, great speed of operation, and don't have to worry about giving distinctive names or identities to numbers of two or more.[6]

Base systems are alternative ways of expressing numbers, but numbers themselves, the abstract denizens of the world behind the glass wall, remain unchanged regardless of the system. The number we write as 49 in the decimal system is the same number in the base-12 (duodecimal) system, in the base-16 (hexadecimal) system, and in the binary system, even though it is written as 41, 31, and 110001 in those respective systems. The decimal system's 49 remains a square number (7×7) and 7 remains a prime number (divisible only by 1 and itself) in whatever system they are written. Numbers—in the world of mathematics—are unaffected by how we choose to name them.

CHAPTER 6

Numbers (II): The Written Form

The development of an efficient base system solved many number problems, but not all. In particular, it didn't solve the problem of how to represent numbers that were to be seen rather than heard. In fact, the decimal base-10 system of counting was fully worked out before the advent of written numbers as we know them today. The problems that had to be solved in order to make written numbers manageable were quite different from the problems involved in constructing a spoken number system.

The leap from spoken to written mathematics is substantial, for entire cultures and for individual learners. Brain and paper together can do what brain alone can't do—not just in making calculations, but in extending what can be done with the number system. Mathematics took off when it was made visible.

Children don't need to invent a new counting system in order to be able to do mathematics on paper (or on a computer), but they do need to discover why written numbers are the way they are, if they are going to use numbers with understanding.

Extending Numbers Spatially

There wouldn't be calculation without visual representation. You can't subtract thirty five from ninety three on your fingers. Simply writing down number words was not a solution. "Ninety three minus thirty five" when written in just that way would be as difficult to calculate on paper as on the fingers or in the head.

To be useful, written mathematics had to have its own distinctive characters and conventions. Once again there were two main problems, neither of which spoken language could help solve. One problem was to find a method of *representing* individual numbers, and the other was to find the best way of *arranging* groups of them spatially.

An early solution to the *representation* problem was to return to tally marks, or rather to modify an ancient practice into a more formal system. The first three Roman numerals I, II, III are obvious replications of notches. In fact, when first inscribed they *were* notches. But it is awkward to count tally marks accurately, even when they are clustered into groups. The number of individual marks can get out of hand quickly. And computation is far inferior to what is possible on the abacus. What is IIIIIII multiplied by IIIIII? (The answer is IIIIIIIIIIIIIIIIIIIIIIIIIIIIIIIIIIIIIIIIII.)

The Roman system used unique symbols for different bases—V for five, X for ten, L for fifty, C for a hundred, D for five hundred, and M for a thousand. The numbers one to ten became I, II, III, IIII, V, VI, VII, VIII, VIIII, X. This is clumsy in the extreme—twenty (two tens) becomes XX, not IIX, which by a different convention becomes eight. (And which requires reading from right to left as well as from left to right in the same system, to determine whether adjacent symbols are to be added or subtracted.) Think of the difficulty of making even a simple calculation, like 17 + 34, which in Roman numerals is XVII + XXXIV, and which for no obvious reason sums to LI. Yet scientists and scholars struggled to use the system for centuries, and with it made some notable calculations in astronomy, geometry, and the construction of trigonometrical tables.

Another alternative was to use letters of the alphabet—in alphabetical order, not as abbreviations of spoken words—for numbers. The Greeks did this and it was a notable advance, because it recognized that the written symbols didn't have to be related to either tally marks or spoken language. They could be unique to the world of mathematics. The Greek letter *epsilon* (ε), for example, fifth letter of the Greek alphabet and therefore the written symbol for the number five, wasn't related to the Greek word for five, or to any sign for five. It was a complete abstraction. But the early Greeks got carried away with this system and, instead of restarting at ten or twelve for a base system, went on until all the letters of the Greek alphabet were exhausted.

Eventually, distinctive characters like 1, 2, 3, 4, 5 evolved, far removed from the alphabetic letters that most of them originally were. They are completely unpredictable from any form of spoken language—just as the signs +, – , and = have no evident relationship to the words "plus," "minus," and "equals."

A New Problem

The base-10 system was adopted from spoken language, so that it was not necessary to have more than 10 distinctive number characters. But there was still the question of how to indicate the size of the groups on any particular occasion, to distinguish, for example, sixty from six hundred or six thousand. The solution was what became known as a *positional* system (or place system).

What happens to written numbers when they get beyond single unit size? How do you represent "ten plus one," "ten plus two," and so forth? What seems obvious to us was by no means obvious to ancient peoples trying to solve the problem. Ignoring for the moment the problem of how to represent ten, should seventeen be written as ten plus seven, or seven plus ten, or a symbol for ten over the top of seven, or what? How could numbers greater than a single digit be indicated, horizontally or vertically, in a consistent manner?[1]

One possible solution was to write numbers out in full, so that three hundred and forty seven would be written as it is spoken:

3 x 100, 4 x 10, 7

It was easy to say such a number—three hundred and forty seven—but a way of writing it was less obvious. For thousands of years people stumbled along with systems involving additional symbols for tens, hundreds, and thousands, so that three hundred and forty seven would be written as three ducks, four fish, and seven, or three squares, four triangles, and seven.

It took brilliant insight to realize that additional symbols for numbers greater than nine were redundant, and that values could be indicated simply by place in a sequence—that three hundred and forty seven could simply be written 347. This dramatic development introduced into mathematical representation not simply economy and relative permanence and portability, but also the concept of order and invariance, not just in the sequence of numbers themselves (1, 2, 3, 4, 5), but also in the manner in which they were written. The number 347 had to be presented spatially in exactly that way, not as 437 or 374.

And even this solution was not as obvious as it first might seem for a left-to-right script. For a start, it could be considered a regressive solution. While the invention of named units like 3 and 7 eliminated the necessity to count individual units—III and IIIIIII—the counting of individual symbols was again required to permit determination of whether a numeral indicated tens, hundreds, thousands, and so on.

And furthermore, the counting had to be done from right to left (to identify "units," tens, hundreds, thousands, and so on), while values were listed from left to right, reflecting the fact that the largest value came first in speech.

Moving into a New Dimension

The place system solved the problem of the representation of numbers greater than nine. But it was still very difficult to calculate with larger numbers, for example, to compute the sum of 5387 and 126. The inspired solution was to move into a second dimension and line numbers up in columns, for example:

$$
\begin{array}{r}
5387 \\
+\ \ \underline{126} \\
= 5513
\end{array}
$$

All this looks obvious to us today (though not to learners), but centuries passed before any culture developed its mathematics with this discovery—that you could do things with numbers if you organized them into columns. And there still remained one major problem, the solution to which was by no means obvious or universal. Indeed, the solution offended many people's beliefs of how mathematics should function.

The Story of 0

So far I have avoided reference to a number "nought," or "zero." I said "four hundred and five" though I had to write 405. I said "ten" and "a hundred" though I wrote 10 and 100. Unless we are literally talking about nothing, the 0 that is so ubiquitous in written numbers never appears in speech. It isn't necessary. It is strictly a written mathematics phenomenon.

What do you do if there are no tens, or hundreds, or thousands, in a number? This is not a problem with speech—you can say "eight hundred and five" without having to pause, cough, or otherwise indicate the absence of any groups of tens. This was also not a problem for writing if everything was spelled out. For example, the number

8 x 100, 5 (for what we would now write as 805)

was just as clear as

8 x 100, 7 x 10, 5 (for 875)

But what could you do when relative position indicated the size of the unit—when the meaning of 875 was recognizable because of the rule that the digit on the right indicated units (in this case 5), the next digit to the left indicated tens (in this case 70), and the next to the left hundreds (800)? How did you indicate the hundreds, tens, and units when there were no tens and units? Various solutions were tried, like leaving a small space for empty groups, distinguishing 8 5 (eight hundred and five) from 85 (eighty-five), or even inserting a marker, like a dash or a square, to indicate a position that wasn't filled (as in 8–5 or 8□5). But this didn't really help, because there was no idea of what to do with the "–" or "□" (or empty space) in calculating. How could these things take the place of numbers?

The solution to all these problems again seems obvious to us today. You put in a zero, which itself acts as a number (so that 5 + 0 equals 5) and

$$\begin{array}{r} 426 \\ \underline{+\ 300} \\ =\ 726 \end{array}$$

The number chain changed at a stroke from

one, two, three, four, five, six, seven, eight, nine, ten

to

zero, one, two, three, four, five, six, seven, eight, nine

written

0, 1, 2, 3, 4, 5, 6, 7, 8, 9

which then recycles

10, 11, 12, 13, 14, 15, 16, 17, 18, 19

and so on through

20, 30, . . . 100, 200 . . .

What to us today seems starkly logical and self-evident was a most difficult concept for earlier cultures to understand, even for their most brilliant mathematicians. It was widely rejected as nonsense, if not illogical and sacrilegious, to have a number that stood for nothing.[2] The whole point about numbers was that they could be paired off with collections of things. How could a number stand for no-thing? What did 0 pair off with? There's a huge glass wall here between the world of mathematics and the physical world.

And in any case, most of the time 0 didn't stand for nothing. It might stand for "no tens" in the number 805, but that is different from the concept of nothing; it doesn't mean not anything, just no tens (or no units, or no hundreds . . .). And how could a number over 100 have no tens in it? It was full of tens. And just like the other numerals, the value of 0 depended on its position. The 0 in 805 had a different meaning from the 0 in 850.

All of this was difficult for ancient mathematicians to grasp, especially as it was widely believed that all numbers had a concrete reality. And if 0 sometimes did act like any other number, for example, in adding 305 and 420, or even—with a conceptual leap—5 and 0, multiplication of 0 or by 0 seemed impossible, or highly illogical and inconsistent. It makes sense that $2 \times 2 = 4$ and that $2 \times 1 = 2$, but what is 2×0? If 2×0 equals nothing, then anything times 0 equals nothing. No other number behaves like that. In multiplication, 0 seems to obliterate everything it comes into contact with. And as for division—divide anything by zero and the answer is unimaginable (so mathematicians declare division by 0 to be illegal!).[3]

Even today, people tend to believe—or to say—that 0 stands for nothing, and that it has the same meaning in the sequence 0, 1, 2, 3 . . . as it does in the numbers 805 or 300. But whatever meaning 0 has, in the abstract world of mathematics, it is not nothing. It is something far more significant than that.

There is in fact a very precise and totally consistent description of what the number 0 is, which is that it is one less than one. It is not one of something less than one of something, which would indeed be nothing of anything, but simply one less than the number one (and therefore an even number). It is a relationship, not a quantity, a something, not a nothing, an essential element in the tautly constructed patterns of the fabric of numbers.

If 0 is such a difficult concept for many adults to handle, historically and today, how must it look to children and other learners? The ancients had to struggle to invent zero to fill well-defined needs in their number systems. But learners today have the opposite task, to discover what are the needs that 0 fills.

I'm not saying that children can't learn to use 0 in simple arithmetic without understanding its relationship to all other numbers. But going through the motions is not understanding. And like many other aspects of mathematical learning without understanding, as a result of repetitive drills and rote memorization—it will make learning and retention much more difficult. It can prove a massive obstacle to the development of further, deeper mathematical understanding.

The Bizarre Realms of the Negative

The number 0 serves one other crucial function. It acts as a bridge or pivot between positive numbers (which extend from 1, 2, 3 . . .) and negative numbers (which extend in the opposite direction from -1, -2, -3 . . .). Negative numbers would never have existed without written mathematics; they are a concept that is completely alien to everyday thought and language.

Together the positive and negative numbers, and 0, are referred to as integers, which means "wholes," in contrast to fractions (which also can be positive and negative).

Negative numbers are a strange crew. They are numbers that run backward—so that not only does the chain of integers have no end, it has no beginning. It is almost impossible to connect negative numbers with intuition and common sense. As recently (mathematically speaking) as 400 years ago, negative numbers were regarded as absurd by major mathematicians.[4] It may be difficult to see how a number (zero) can stand for nothing, but it is even harder to see how a number less than zero can stand for a negative quantity, or how one "negative" quantity can be bigger or smaller than another.

Usually no reason is given for the existence of negative numbers; students simply are told that negative numbers exist and that they should learn about such numbers.

The most common way of explaining negatives in mathematics instruction is with reference to financial debt—negative quantities stand for what you owe rather than what you possess. If you try to subtract one amount from a smaller amount, you go "into the red" with a negative number. If, for example, you have 6 dollars and spend 8 dollars (or if you move eight numbers to the left on the number line), you end up with -2 ("minus two" or "negative two") dollars.[5]

But in the debt example, we basically are dealing only with positive numbers—subtracting one positive number from another, with a positive difference between them. There's no such thing as a negative dollar. You owe a positive number of dollars. And subtracting negatives is another matter altogether. If you try to deduct negative 6 (-6) from 3, the mathematical result is 9, which means that you finish up with more than you started with. This makes sense mathematically, but in no other way.

To calculate 3 – (-6), as in the preceding example, it is necessary to employ the strange but familiar rule that two negatives make a positive (though two wrongs don't make a right), which we all learned, probably with minimal comprehension, in school.

The mathematical concept of negative numbers gets complicated with mixtures of positives and negatives, and of negatives with negatives.

Subtract a negative from a positive and the result (as we have just seen) is a larger positive: 3 – (-6) = 9. Subtract a negative from a negative and the result is a larger number that may be positive, negative, or zero; for example (-3) – (-6) = 3; (-4) – (-2) = -2, and (-4) – (-4) = 0

And matters go completely haywire (conceptually, though not mathematically) with multiplication and division. Multiply two positive numbers and the result, reasonably enough, is another positive number: 3 × 6 = 18. But multiply two negatives and the result is also positive: (-3) × (-6) = 18. A negative result occurs only when one of the two numbers to be multiplied is negative, and then it doesn't matter which of the two it is: (-3) × 6 = -18 and 3 × (-6) = -18.

Divide one negative number by another negative number and the result is positive: (-6) ÷ (-3) = 2. But when one of the two quantities is positive and the other negative, the result is negative: (-6) ÷ 3 = -2 and 6 ÷ (-3) = -2. None of this can be explained through nonmathematical demonstrations; it can be learned only by rule, and understood only through mathematics—if the learner doesn't hit the glass wall first.

Even in mathematical terminology and notation, there are ambiguities and confusions over negation. The word "minus" and the - sign are employed as verbs for the operation of subtraction, and sometimes also as adjectives to designate negative quantity[6] ("minus three" and -3). This is the reason I put parentheses around numbers in some of my earlier discussions, hoping that (4) – (-4) was a bit clearer than 4 – -4.

It is only because negative numbers exist that the counting numbers, the numbers we normally deal with, are referred to as "positive." (Pity the inquisitive student who asks why some numbers are positive; the only answer is to distinguish them from the intrusive negatives.) Because of the confusion that negative numbers can cause, positive numbers sometimes must be clearly denoted as such—not just as 4, but as +4—so that it is sometimes necessary to write such things as 4 + (+4). On other occasions the + sign may be said to be understood, so that what we think of as 2 + 2 = 4 is "really" (+2) + (+2) = (+4).

Negatives behave in surprising and sometimes uncontrollable ways. They probably have caused more headaches to mathematical beginners and to mathematical experts than any other mathematical form. You can't tell if a positive number is the result of the multiplication of two positives or two negatives, which can be confusing and inconvenient. Why don't you get something other than a positive number when two negatives are multiplied or divided? Because there is mathematically nothing else for them to be.

Perhaps most surprising is that despite the confusion caused by negatives, and their doubtful utility, it often should be considered so important to teach them in their full complexity. I can't imagine that many people became mathematicians because of their fascination with negatives, no matter how negative their views might be about education or the world in general.

WAS MATHEMATICS EVER WITHOUT TEARS?

Histories of mathematics tend to make the development of our basic ideas about numbers sound graceful and uncomplicated. I see different scenarios.

I see an ancient shepherd, or whoever it was, trying desperately to convince his friends that one pebble stood for one sheep while they shook their heads with about as much understanding as the sheep themselves. I see the shepherd trying to point out three sheep, while his friends wondered if he was referring to sheep who always stood in the corner or sheep who were lame in one leg. I see his friends losing patience when the shepherd pointed to two groups of sheep and claimed that one was three and the other four—until a sheep wandered from one group to another, and the groups became two and five.

Imagine the first struggles to give *names* to individual pebbles, or to individual fingers, among people who scarcely gave names to each other. And the pebble that was named "one" on one occasion might be "two" on other. How did anyone grasp let alone explain that numbers always had to be in the same order, when numerical order itself was a nebulous and unfamiliar concept? How many numbers had to be invented before people got the idea that numbering could go on for ever? Did counting lurch from two to three to four, perhaps at the rate of one number a generation, or one a century, until it took off like a rocket when people realized there was no end to the process, at which point a whole new cluster of problems arose.

I see enormous conflict between one group who preferred to count with pebbles and another group who thought it only natural to count with notches. I see misunderstandings and conflict between groups who preferred to count with one base system rather than another, or to write with one place system rather than another. I see enthusiasts prepared to beat or banish adherents of "deviant" numerical practices. I see priests trying to keep their mathematical secrets to themselves, businessmen trying to steal the holy technologies for commercial purposes, and administrators and bureaucrats trying to organize everyone in the same way—and to tax them into the bargain. I can't even bring myself to contemplate the plight of teachers in those mathematically tumultuous times, not to mention all those people who thought numbers were a faddish and unnecessary indulgence that the economy couldn't afford, or who said they just didn't have a mathematical brain.

And all this would have gone on for centuries. Early humanity didn't stumble over the fundamental aspects of the number system, the way everything mathematical seems to lie conveniently to hand for us today. More than insights and ingenuity were required; enormous amounts of tact, determination, perseverance, politicking, despair, and even bloodshed must have been involved.

And when I think of all of this, I have even more respect for the child who sorts out "the basics" in a few short years, "helped" by adults who feel certain that everything about numbers is straightforward and self-evident in the first place.

CHAPTER 7

Labeling, Ordering, and Quantifying

"Number" is a word with a number of meanings, not all of them mathematical. Sometimes the word is used simply to refer to a distinctive shape, for example, a mark on a piece of paper. Alternative terms for numbers in this sense, when we are referring merely to the marks, are *numerals* and *digits*. We write the numerals 1, 3, and 7 when we want to write the number 137.

The marks have familiar names (like "one," "two," "three," "four") but the names mean nothing beyond whatever is identified by the mark itself. "Four," in such circumstances, means the numeral 4—when, for example, I ask a painter to put "four" on my door, or go into a hardware store and say, "I'd like to buy a four and two sevens, please." And that is all.

Many uses have been found for numbers that are not mathematical. The physical world is full of numbers that look as if they are doing something mathematical, but they are aliens smuggled across the border to do nonmathematical work that could very well be done by local resources. Such numbers are used as identification tags or labels, and the only meaning they have comes from whatever they are attached to. They might just as well be letters of the alphabet.

LABELING

Numbers that refer to nothing more than the object they are attached to are said to be *categorical*—they label a category, or an instance of a category. The numerals commonly placed on the back of athletes' uniforms are categorical numbers. The number on the shirt of a hockey player tells us nothing except who that player is. If the number tells us anything else about the player who wears it, that is because of something we know about the individual, not about the number.

The "Proper" Use of Numbers

In essence, the number on the back of an athlete's shirt functions like a proper noun. Grammarians make a special category in language for "proper nouns" (like the names of people, places, and ships). They doubt whether proper nouns should be considered words at all, in a linguistic sense, because they have no meaning, not in the sense of a definition. That is the reason proper nouns do not appear in most dictionaries. It makes no sense to say, "How do you define John F. Kennedy?" John F. Kennedy refers to the historical person (or to a ship or school or public building with the same name), and nothing else. If I tell you that my friend's name is George Jones, I am telling you nothing about him except that his name is George Jones.

Grammarians say that proper nouns have reference but no sense. They denote but do not connote. And this is the way numbers (or numerals) behave when they are used categorically. They have no meaning beyond the person or object they are attached to; they have reference but no sense. Perhaps they should be called "proper numbers," no more a meaningful part of mathematics than proper nouns are a meaningful part of language. The similarity of categorical numbers to more meaningful kinds of numbers, like the similarity of proper nouns to more meaningful words, is coincidental.

The vast majority of numbers that surround us in our daily lives are categorical, or primarily categorical. Their very familiarity inhibits our recognizing them for what they are, numbers without meaning. We don't need any "number sense" for numbers used categorically.

Numbers are placed on the backs of athletes for easier identification, because numbers are often (but not always) bigger and easier to read than names. Letters of the alphabet would serve just as well, in fact more economically. The numbers 1 to 9, singly and in pairs, will distinguish among only 99 players, while the letters A to Z, singly and in pairs, would distinguish among 702 individuals. In contrast to numbers, however, letters may appear to be meaningful for players labeled OK, US, or other combinations too suggestive to mention.

Nothing arithmetical can be done with numerals used in a categorical manner—you can't say that player number 36 is three times better than player number 12, or that team 4 has twice as many players as team 2. The numbers can't be combined or compared with each other; they make no mathematical sense. Numbers on backs are not the same as numbers on the scoreboard.

Many of the numbers we encounter most in our daily lives are categorical in function, or might just as well be: the numbers on buses, vehicle license plates, admission tickets, lottery tickets, and books in libraries. We can't do anything mathematical with these numbers—it makes no sense to add them together, or take their square roots.

The "serial numbers" on manufactured products are basically categorical identification numbers; they may mean something to the manufacturers, but not to anyone else. My computer is number BX 4628; I doubt if that means I have anything in common with the owner of BX 4627, or that my machine is twice as good as BX 2314. Just about everything has an identification number these days, from radios and microwave ovens to automobiles and airplanes—and, of course, people. Individuals have social security numbers, work identification numbers, credit card numbers, bank account numbers, and "personal identification numbers" for communicating with machines instead of with people. None of these numbers has any meaning, mathematical or otherwise.

ORDERING

Sometimes, however, meaning can be derived from categorical numbers because of the systematic way they are employed. If we walk a block from 42nd Street and find ourselves on 43rd Street, it is a reasonable bet that we are heading in the direction of 44th Street, even if there are intervening streets with names rather than numbers so that we can't calculate exactly how many streets separate us from our destination. The numbers on the spines of library books indicate where they are placed relative to each other on the shelves, even though the numbers may not be consecutive. If we have ticket 47 in a line up, we know we are ahead of someone with ticket 56 but behind someone with ticket 32, even if some people have taken more than one ticket and others have thrown their tickets away and left. We know someone born in 1948 is older than someone born in 1963, even if we don't bother to calculate the difference in years. We can draw these conclusions because we are familiar with *numerical order.*

Putting Order into Numbers

The reason numbers functioning categorically may carry a meaning beyond the mere labeling of an object or location is that they can be allocated in a consistent manner, in the order of the number chant. By respecting the conventional order of numbers, we can employ them in a variety of meaningful ways. The numbers are still allocated categorically, but they can be used to indicate relative position in time and space. They become ordinal (meaning "orderly").

Numerical order enables us to organize and contrast every kind of object and event—we can say that something is more than, less than, or equal to something else, in age, size, weight, rank, loudness, proximity in time, proximity in space, quantity, quality, and any other attribute we care to consider. The possibility of using numbers in this orderly manner is an enormous source of power, available because we can recite, and endlessly construct, numbers in a serial order that practically everyone knows and no one disputes. We may want to rebel against the way numerical (or alphabetical) order is used, but no one ever claims that the world would be a better place if 7 came before 3 (or M before G in the alphabet).

Numerical order is not found in the physical world, except when we put it there. There is no "order" in the natural world because there are no numbers there. The notion of order—with the associated ideas of "more than," "less than," and "the same as"—comes from our fertile brain.

There is no way anyone can tell us what order is; we need to understand order to understand the explanation. There is no way anyone can *show* us what order is; without prior understanding, the demonstration is meaningless. Order doesn't reside in objects but in relationships. We can't look at a tree standing alone and see that it has a property of being taller, greener, or nearer. Nothing comes with order inherent in it, including numbers. We may learn numbers in conventional order in the form of the number chant, but the idea or concept of order that we associate with numbers, we must put there ourselves. We provide the sense of order that enables numbers to be organized "numerically." And from the organization of numbers, we can create organization in the rest of our world.

We are no longer allocating numbers arbitrarily to objects and events, as we do with the categorical use of numbers, if we put them into some kind of order. We are allocating objects and events to numbers, to a structure in our own mind. The numbers, literally, rule.

The Creative Use of Numerical Order

The establishment of an invariant order in which to say numbers, and to think about them, may seem a modest achievement, but it facilitates a great part of the organization of our daily lives. The ordinal use of numbers—systematic application without calculation—in our society is vast.

Even so, numerical order probably takes second place in our daily lives (note the ordinal expression) to alphabetical order, where there is clearly no relationship to quantities. Order is enormously important in bureaucratically organized cultures, and has made possible much of contemporary society itself. Imagine the chaos of our libraries, dictionaries, encyclopedias, telephone books, atlases, and street directories, not to mention address lists and tax rolls, without alphabetical order.

But a dramatic revolution is taking place. The value of alphabetical and numerical order has diminished and may soon disappear, certainly as far as computers are concerned. Electronic searches can proceed so rapidly through huge data bases that there is no advantage to storing individual items in alphabetical or numerical order.

Order Without Distance or Direction

When numbers or letters are used in their conventional and predictable order, everything can be put into a place from which it can be rapidly retrieved. But ordinal numbers can't be used for calculation because they don't have to be consecutive, or to begin from a fixed point. When you take a number in a waiting room or delicatessen to indicate your turn to be served, it doesn't matter which number began the series, only how many people are ahead of you. In competitive ice skating there is a maximum score of 6, but no one ever gets zero unless they are absent or disqualified. It doesn't matter where the numbering begins—it can be 0 or 1, or any other number below the maximum of six.

The fact that a number "nothing" is not required for numerical order is one reason for the centuries of puzzlement and controversy before zero could be admitted into the mathematical community. People rarely start with 0 if you ask them to count to five or ten.

It is not necessary for numbers used ordinally to run "up" from 1 (or 0) to 10, or to some other maximum. The numbers could just as well run "down"—the order is just as dependable. There is no logical direction in which ordinal numbers have to go. Many games count "backward" (like darts, which generally runs from 501 or 301 to 0). The "countdown" for spacecraft launches employs numbers in reverse order. We may *say* that some numbers are "bigger" or "higher" than others, that 17 is "higher" than 14, but that is just a conventional way of talking about numbers. When numbers are used for ordinal purposes, higher doesn't necessarily have priority or greater value. Try telling someone who is "Number One" in a competitive event that it is less than 2 or 3.

Often not all the numbers available between the two ends of a sequence are used. There may be quite arbitrary gaps, for example, in the scoring for tennis, where "points" jump from 0 ("love") to 15, 30, and 40, and then if necessary to simple successions of winning plays. Bridge allocates points for tricks in multiples of 10, starting at 20, and advances with various bonuses, penalties, and game scores in multiples of 50, with the result that scores of thousands can be made. Many other sports and card games allocate points in an incremental (or decremental) but otherwise arbitrary manner. Some competitive contests (like boxing, diving, and gymnastics) allocate scores in the form of decimal fractions.

QUANTIFYING

One can think of the number system as a chain with an infinite number of links, or an endless string of pearls, or a limitless succession of bricks or pebbles, or in other metaphorical ways, but none of these descriptions should be taken literally. An actual chain or sequence of pearls or bricks could not by itself constitute a number system. A pearl (or brick) in one place could always be substituted for one in another place, and that is not the case with numbers. We have to talk about numbers metaphorically because they have no tangible existence. We infuse *number* into objects (or sounds, or measuring units) when we relate ideas of numerosity to them, just as we infuse *order* into them. And all for two reasons:

1. because each whole number is exactly one more than the one before it, and
2. because we (sometimes) can lay our number system on the world, and objects we envelop in this way can become infused with the relational properties of the numbers themselves.

We make three pencils and two pencils equal five pencils.

The Fundamental Relationship Among Numbers

A crucial difference between the number system and the alphabet is that while letters of the alphabet are essentially unrelated to each other—it wouldn't matter if they were arbitrarily reorganized into a different order, except for confounding everything we have arranged alphabetically—numbers are locked into an immutable pattern of relationships. This includes the numbers that we have never yet used, or even thought of.

We could not count "one, two, three, five, four" the way the alphabet could be "A, B, C, E, D"—not without changing the meaning of "five" and "four" so that "five" would mean everything that "four" now means and "four" would take the place of "five." This is because there is a locked-in set of relationships among numbers that doesn't exist among letters of the alphabet.

Each number[1] is exactly one more than the one before it. This is not a matter of space, though numbers often are discussed as if they were equidistant segments on a line—for example when we say that six is halfway between four and eight. This, again, is metaphorical. The distance between numbers exists only in terms of numbers themselves. Six is halfway between four and eight *mathematically*; it wouldn't matter if the numerals were of physically different sizes, and physically different distances apart, such as:

4 **6** **8**

Every whole number is more than the number that precedes it, and therefore less than the number that follows it. This is a simple matter of language.

But to be precise (and mathematical), every number is exactly *one* more than its predecessor and exactly *one* less than its successor. All the other properties of numbers and mathematics follow from this fundamental relationship. Since three is one more than two, and four is one more than three, four has to be two more than two—in fact, four is "twice" two. Every number knows its place precisely. As soon as we make this progression from one number to the next *precise*, each step is *exactly* one, then we are on the other side of the glass wall, in the world of mathematics.

Why is every element in the number sequence always "one" more than its predecessor, and one less than the number that follows it? What is this "one," so that three is exactly one "one" more than two, and four is two "ones" more than two, all neatly interlocking, interrelated, and endlessly predictable? The answer every time is the fundamental cognitive and natural language distinction of the singular. While plural—by definition—can be anything more than one, singular, also by definition, is a whole, a unit, an item, an entity in itself—it is literally "singular." Nothing can be less than one and remain whole. Nothing can be more than one and remain singular. In the words of a traditional song, "One is one and all alone and ever more shall be so." By making plurality an ordered succession of singularities, we make number.

Whole numbers are an endless parade of "ones," each with a unique name and its ordered and lawful place. The endless progression is based on that single distinction, a progression that turns out to be full of beautiful, unexpected, and useful relationships.

We do not find numbers in the physical world. We have to put them there. But numbers are also not in our head (unless we recite them to ourselves, or do "mental arithmetic," which is no more "mental" than arithmetic done on paper, except that we talk silently to ourselves). Number is an unrealized idea in our heads until it is manifested in the basic form of the number sequence, which becomes a material that can be manipulated the way a carpenter manipulates wood.

The manipulation of numbers that we can do in our heads is limited. There is just so much working memory and "computing space" available to the brain, and only the most simple calculations can be done in spoken language, aloud or silently. But with the help of notational systems—the visual representations of numbers and of manipulations of numbers—mathematical calculations of vast complexity (extending sometimes beyond any one person's lifetime) can be accomplished, on paper and on computers. Notational systems, which have a history predating the invention of any other form of written language, help us to do things with the number sequence, but they do not make the sequence possible in the first place. What gives birth to the number sequence, and to its endless possibilities, is the childhood chant.

Counting—with a Purpose

Some meanings of the verb to count are clearly metaphorical, for example, when we say that certain people "count" because they are prominent or influential members of a community or group. We say we can count on someone, or that a mistake doesn't count, or that we can't count on fine weather tomorrow. Another meaning of to count, already discussed, is to produce the number chant. We say we teach children to "count" when we teach them to recite the number words, up to about ten or twelve or twenty. We teach them a little more about counting in that sense when we teach them the combinatory rules—how "twenty one" and "twenty two" follow twenty, and how "thirty one" and "thirty two" follow thirty. Children can learn to say these words without attaching any meaning to what they say. The word "counting" is used in this essentially meaningless sense when we sometimes are asked to "count backward," or to count to a hundred while someone hides. There is nothing mathematical about such activities.

But the verb "to count" is also transitive; we can count *things.* Instead of simply saying, "one, two, three . . . ," we can count, "one finger, two fingers, three fingers . . . ," or "one pencil, two pencils, three pencils . . . ." We can reckon, tally (in a numerical sense), total, and quantify. We can lay the number sequence over objects in the world in a meaningful way, even before we engage in any mathematical calculations. This is using a number as an adjective instead of as a noun or a pronoun. But a number is very different from any other adjective. To say there are five apples is a very different thing from saying there are green apples. Fiveness is not a property of apples the way greenness is, or even heaviness or taste. None of these things changes if you put one more apple in the group.

By saying there are five apples, the apples become imbued with fiveness. They assimilate all the properties of five (which is the reason people think it is obvious that five apples demonstrate the number five). To say there are five apples means they have the same properties, numerically, as the number five, that one more will make six, and two more, seven.

Counting in this sense is a complex act, involving:

- knowing—or being able to construct—the number sequence, at least up to the number of objects to be counted,
- understanding that successive numbers must be allocated once and only once to each of the objects to be counted,
- understanding that the order in which the objects are numbered is irrelevant, although the order of the numbers themselves must be respected,
- finally, understanding that the total number of objects (itself a complex concept) is indicated by the last number used in the counting sequence.

Complicated all this might be, but while children usually learn parrot-wise to *recite* the number chant before they are able to do anything with it, they sometimes also demonstrate an understanding of the complexities of *tallying* before they have fully learned the number chant. They may "count" a group of objects in front of them with a sequence such as

one, two, five, seven, three

finishing perhaps with something like "twenty-twelve," and even achieving the final step of declaring that the total number of objects is "twenty-twelve," or whatever the last number was that they reached. They respect, even if they don't fully understand, the "cardinality" principle.

The notion of "how many" is not easy to grasp. "More" is much easier. Children when they begin to use numbers—when they have worked out that some numbers are "larger" than others—typically "count" quite erratically. Any number of objects beyond two or three becomes four, or seven, or some other arbitrary number. Counting is literally "one, two, a lot . . . ." Children have related the idea of quantity to numbers, but not in any precise manner. But counting is very complicated—a considerable intellectual achievement that took the human race thousands of years to master.

Numerosity

Counting in the totaling or quantifying sense requires a new concept—that of numerosity, or quantity—that cannot be understood from explanation or demonstration. By using our string of numbers, we can say that there are "five" people, or "seven" people, in a group, and that a group of seven people is "more than" a group of five. But what do these numbers mean? The number five doesn't mean a group or total of five people, or five objects, or anything else in the world. Totals don't exist in the world. They are again products of our brain.[2]

Every number has a mathematical meaning, of course. Or to be precise, any number of mathematical meanings, providing it is not being used categorically. Ten means twice five, or nine plus one, or eleven minus one, and so forth. But psychologically, the meaningfulness of numbers is limited. Only the first few numbers have any specific meaning; after that, the only meaning that individual numbers have outside mathematics is for greater or lesser amounts of "more."

There are indications of a substantial cognitive discontinuity beyond four, when numbers leave the world of perceptual experience and function solely in the world of mathematics. For example, children at the age of three may be able to recite the number chant up to ten or more in the conventional order, but they can't *count* more than two or three objects without getting confused.[3]

Even at the age of five, when they may be able to count to 20 or more (in the reciting sense), children can find counting objects (in the tallying sense) difficult beyond the number four. Their understanding is confined to the familiar world of objects and events, and they haven't crossed the threshold into the world of mathematics.

The difficulty that children may experience in entering the world of mathematics is particularly notable in contrast to their competence with language. By the age of six, children may be able to use and understand 14,000 words.[4] But the language competence they have gained is not all-embracing. Difficulty persists with words referring to ways of viewing the world that they still do not fully understand, for example with *time*, not just with clock and calendar time, but with concepts like soon, shortly, never, always, and sometimes.[5] (Yet they may be expected to understand the two times table.)

A Limit to the Imagination

We tend to think that numbers used as totals are meaningful because they tell us things about the world. We value ten dollars more than five dollars because we know that ten dollars is "more." But the meaningfulness comes from the way we understand numbers; it proceeds from the mind to the world, not from the world to the mind. As I described in Chapter 4, it is impossible to see, or to imagine, more than four or five of anything, in a numerical sense. We can imagine larger groups, of course, and we can imagine, very roughly, the approximate size of larger groups, but we cannot think about their actual quantity without going into mathematical relationships.

Numbers are not like sounds, where we can hear that one sound is louder than another, or higher in pitch, or different in timbre. They are not like color, or temperature, or weight, or size, where our senses can tell us that something is more than something else. Numerosity is totally abstract.

The power we gain from employing numbers is never-ending—even if we never fully comprehend the numbers that we finish up with. Mathematics helps us to create a physical world that would not otherwise exist. A spool of numbers is always available for us to spin and unwind, not just to count, but to compute. We can add and subtract, multiply and divide, and we can elaborate upon numbers in a seemingly infinite variety of ways. We can calculate and measure.

CHAPTER 8

Calculating and Measuring

Once a functional number system was in place in speech and writing, people could compare magnitudes, a practical and intellectual accomplishment far beyond anything that language could achieve. They could, for example, compare whether the total of sheep, ships or coconuts they had today was more or less than (or the same as) the total they had yesterday, or hoped to have tomorrow, and more or less than (or the same as) the total that someone else possessed. The totals were mathematical; they were in the form of numbers, and they could be exact as well as indisputable. But the *comparisons* remained nonmathematical—"more" or "less" are words and concepts in everyday language, and not (in these instances) precise mathematical terms. We can say that nine is more than six the way we might say that a gale is more than a light breeze; it's information without exactitude.

But people learned to do other things with numbers that make comparisons of totals both mathematical and precise. They learned to *calculate.* Instead of merely saying that nine is *more* than six, they could put a number to the difference, and compute that nine is precisely *three* more than six. They could do this without further counting. They could also calculate that nine and six together make a new total of fifteen, again without further counting. Such reasoning moved counting deep into the world of mathematics.

CALCULATION

Calculating takes off where counting stops, ascending into realms undreamed of outside mathematics. The number system, for all its essential simplicity, is wondrously productive. First it enables you to count, then to calculate, and finally to calculate so that counting is no longer necessary.

Calculation is everything you can do with numbers without counting. It even enables you to do things with numbers where counting would be impossible, either because the counting would be beyond the time or skill you have available, or because some of the numbers you need would not be available through counting. If numbers are regarded as notes on an endless musical scale, calculation would be the never-ending possibilities of operas, ballets, and symphonies.

What made calculation not only possible, but precise, dependable, and infinitely productive? The answer is explorations of the ways in which numbers are related to each other. Numbers are tightly enmeshed in an infinite network of relationships existing only among themselves. They are like knots in a fishing net. Without the net individual knots would not exist, and without the knots the net would not exist. Every knot is incontestably linked to every other knot in the net.

Every number is related to every other number, actually or potentially, in innumerably different ways. And these relationships are eternally binding. Nothing could be more intuitively appealing than the relationships that numbers have with each other because they perfectly reflect the three basic characteristics—the three Cs—that human beings expect to find in a stable world. Numbers are *consistent* because 9 + 6 always equals 15, no matter where and when the calculation is made. They are *coherent* because no other calculation or arrangement of numbers can affect the fact that 9 + 6 = 15. And there is *consensus* because no one can argue that for them personally, 9 + 6 doesn't equal 15. Numbers and calculations may not always map neatly on to the physical world, or demonstrate consistency, coherence, and consensus when they are laid upon that world, but that is always because of indeterminacies in the world. Numbers are always reliable, though the uses to which they are put may not be.

Mathematics often is taught by showing learners what can be done *with* numbers instead of helping them to discover the number system itself, putting the cart before the horse. Demonstrations that two of something and three of something make five of something mean nothing without the understanding that five is the inevitable value[1] of the mathematical relationship of 2 + 3. Novices may learn by rote to perform a few basic mathematical rituals, but there will be no mathematical insight.

Relationships and "Operations"

Without relationships, pairs of numbers mean nothing. Their only meaning lies in their relationships. That I have nine dollars in change and you have six means little beyond the fact that I have more than you; they are two unrelated scraps of information. What the numbers mean is how they are related, to each other and to other numbers. The joint "meaning" of the nine that is the total of my dollars and the six that is the total of yours depends on how they are related.

If we combine the 9 and the 6, which is the relationship signaled by the plus sign (+), their joint meaning is 15. If we are interested in the mathematical difference between the 9 and the 6, which is the relationship signaled by the minus sign (–), their joint meaning is 3. The meaning of our joint 15 dollars if we want to buy something costing 17 dollars is that we are 2 dollars short. The meaning of any two numbers is another number.

The various ways in which relationships among numbers are uncovered and calculations made are referred to typically as "operations," like the basic quartet that most people are familiar with—addition, subtraction, multiplication, and division. But the word *operation* also can be mystifying for beginners. "Operation" (or operator) has a different meaning in mathematical language than natural language might suggest.

Addition, for example, is not an operation in the sense of doing something to anything. We aren't doing anything to numbers when we say that two and two are four, any more than we are doing anything to Paris and France when we say that Paris is the capital of France. We're just expressing a fact. Nothing has been done to anything.

THE ENDLESSLY MEANINGFUL RELATIONSHIPS OF NUMBERS

Throughout this book I describe the fundamental relationship that lies at the heart of the number system—the fact that one more than one has the name two, one more than two has the name three, one more than three has the name four, and so on. The "one more than the preceding number" relationship gets the number system started, keeps it going, and ensures that there is potentially no end. Counting can go on forever.

But with endless counting come endless other possibilities, starting with the fact that we can count (and calculate) the number of numbers between one number and another. Sixteen is one more than 15, but it is also two more than 14, and ten more than 6, and so on. Sixteen is also four less than 20, and 1000 less than 1016. If you count to 16 twice, you encounter a total of 32 numbers. If you count only halfway to 16, you encounter just 8. These are enduring verities.

Some elementary relationships are expressed by the familiar signs of mathematical "operators":

relationship		value	mathematical name of relationship
16 + 2	=	18	addition
16 – 2	=	14	subtraction
16 x 2	=	32	multiplication
16 ÷ 2	=	8	division

and the less familiar

16^2	=	256	exponent (in this case, "square")
$\sqrt{16}$	=	4	root (in this case, "square root")

and a multitude of others.

There is also an infinity of ways in which different combinations of numerals can have the same mathematical value, for example

$16 = 14 + 2$ (and also $13 + 3$, $12 + 4$ . . .)
$16 = 18 - 2$ (and also $19 - 3$, $20 - 4$ . . .)
$16 = 8 \times 2$ (and also 4×4, 2×8 . . .)
$16 = 32 \div 2$ (and also $48 \div 3$, $64 \div 4$ . . .)
$16 = 4^2$ (and also 2^4 . . .)
$16 = \sqrt{256}$ (and also $\sqrt[3]{4096}$, $\sqrt[4]{65{,}536}$ . . .)

In addition, by virtue of the fact that they are all equivalent to 16, we can say that $(14 + 2)$, $(18 - 2)$, (8×2), $(32 \div 2)$, (4^2), and $(\sqrt{256})$ are all equivalent to each other, and also to $(13 + 3)$, $(19 - 3)$, (4×4), $(48 \div 3)$, (2^4), $(\sqrt[3]{4096})$, and endless other possibilities. There is no limit to the ways in which numbers relate to each other. For variety and dependability, there is nothing like it on earth.

Mathematical Meanings

I discussed in Chapter 3 how "add," "subtract," "multiply," "divide," and "equals" don't mean the same in everyday situations as they do in mathematics, and the words and phrases used to explain these technical terms don't reflect what happens in mathematics.

Mathematically, as I've just suggested, *addition* can be regarded as a direction to a particular point in numerical space, representing the combination[2] of two magnitudes. Many children seem able to intuit this before they have mastered their "addition" tables. Asked to add four and three, they start from four and "count-on" the next three numbers on their fingers—"five, six, *seven*." They don't find the answer on their fingers; they use their fingers to help them reach the number they are looking for. The fingers are a shortcut to a number, which is not the same as being told that three pencils and two pencils make five pencils. Counting-on achieves its purpose in the world of numbers—for a short time at least. In the long run it can be seriously misleading, as I explain in Chapter 13.

Mathematically speaking, the word *multiply* signals another particular relationship among numbers. The value of this relationship is the number that would be reached by combining[3] numerical magnitudes of the same size. Thus the value of 7×4 is the number that would be reached by combining seven magnitudes of four (or four magnitudes of seven), which could be achieved rather laboriously by counting-on. The value of 438×897 is the number that would be reached by combining 438 magnitudes of 897. No one would ever want to do this by counting-on, of course, because mathematics provides easier ways of calculating the value of numbers in multiplicative relationships.

Mathematically, the value of 5 – 2 (*subtraction*) is the distance between magnitudes of 5 and 2. This numerical distance can be determined by counting-on (another occasional strategy of children) from 2 to 5, or by counting-back from 5 to 2, but only for relatively small whole numbers. There is no "taking away." The fact that 5 – 2 = 3 is merely one alternative way of saying that 2 + 3 = 5. Nothing has changed except the point of view, the particular relationship focused upon.

And what is the *division* relationship? The expression 18 ÷ 3 = 6 is perhaps best seen as another way of viewing the relationship 6 × 3 = 18, a complement rather than an opposite. In the network of numbers, six is the magnitude you would combine three times to reach eighteen (and three is the number you would combine six times for the same value). Division is not the inverse of anything. It is just another relationship. It is the partition of a magnitude into a number (not necessarily a whole number) of smaller magnitudes of equal size.

Finally, the *equals* (=) sign in mathematics signposts an alternative means of stating a value or expression. The expression 9 + 6 = 15 means that 15 is the value of 9 + 6. The expression 9 + 6 = 10 + 5 means that 9 + 6 has the same value as 10 + 5; the two sides of any equation are always equivalent and substitutable in a mathematical context.

The differences between the meaning of words in mathematical language and natural language don't entail that the mathematical meanings aren't learnable. The mathematical meanings can be comprehended, but only in the world of mathematics, which is where they belong. The way mathematical "operations" or relationships are discussed in everyday language can be only a rough metaphorical approximation for the mathematical state of affairs, and like all metaphors can be understood only if the recipient is familiar with the allusion. For someone without the mathematics, the metaphor can be more confusing than helpful.

Children (and older people) can even learn to go through the motions of performing the rituals of simple mathematical tasks without understanding what they are doing mathematically. But without the intuition, they soon hit the glass wall, and become frustrated and impatient.

MEASUREMENT

The number system is extraordinarily versatile and useful, but there is only one thing it is good for when laid over the physical world, and that is counting.

Without counting, nothing useful can be done with the number system beyond simple labeling and categorizing. Numbers alone can't be used to measure, record, compare, or predict. People who wanted to do anything *practical* with the number system—with mathematics—had to count. And to count, you need something countable. You need units.

Sometimes the units can be quite abstract. Numbers themselves are the ultimate units. When you say that four plus six equals ten, then you are saying (in effect) that four units and six units equal ten units. Units of what? Units of number. Magnitudes. But calculations aren't usually made in the abstract, simply as a juggling of numbers, except by those two singular categories of individuals, professional mathematicians and hapless schoolchildren.

Usually, calculations are about some aspect of the world to which people want to apply the power and convenience of mathematics. And when that was the case in the past, self-contained and unambiguously countable units had to be found—or invented. Each individual unit had to be clearly distinguishable and separable from every other unit. In effect, a string of numbers was laid over a string of countable objects, paired off one by one, so that calculations could be performed with the numbers as if they were being performed on the objects to which the numbers were linked.

Often the countable units are so obvious that we take them for granted. If we are counting heads, or sheep, or dollars, then these—self-evidently—are the units we are counting. We don't give the nature of the unit itself a second thought. Unit and number are treated as one.

But sometimes a unit is not self-evident; it doesn't exist in the nature of whatever it is we want to apply our mathematics to. And in that case a unit must be invented. We have to construct something we can count. We need a *measure.* Most human achievements that involve mathematics, from mundane buying and selling to complex organization and engineering, would have been impossible without the invention of units (or *measures*) that could be counted.

And the invention of countable units often has been difficult, requiring not just ingenuity but also communal acceptance and agreement. In many cases practical and reliable units continue to evade us, as in the search for measures of beauty, excellence, intelligence, or human worth.

Slicing Up Space and Time

Space and time don't come to us in handy units, neatly prepackaged for our mathematical convenience. Space and time are as free of natural boundaries as the surface of the open ocean. Units that seem so obvious to us now, like inches, yards, and miles (or centimeters, meters and kilometers), and minutes, days, and years, all had to be invented, quite arbitrarily, though often with an eye on significant natural phenomena. These units also had to be disseminated and agreed upon, which wasn't always easy.

Finding a unit of measurement for *distance* is not as self-evident as we might casually think. It must have been a huge problem for the ancients. You see a mountain on the skyline, or a tree on the other side of a river, or a roof that needs some kind of support. There are no obvious intermediate objects or indicators that you can use to count how far away something is—the way you can use numbers to count how far 9 is from 6. There is no self-evident way to calculate the length, breadth, height, or distance of objects. You can say perhaps that a child's head reaches no higher than the shoulder of an adult, but you can't say how much taller that adult is than the child. You can't say that a tree is seventeen sheep away.

As the Greek mathematician Pythagorus said, there is one thing that is a measure of all things—the human body. The basic units of distance are—or were—the inch (the size of the thumb—the French word for inch is *pouce*, which is also the French word for thumb), the foot (the approximate size of an adult male foot), the yard (approximately the size of a pace), and the mile (which originally meant a thousand—mille—paces). Establishing all of this required considerable agreement (or legislation), and usually a good deal of politicking as well. It is one thing to decide that one standard unit of distance should be a thumb's width, and another standard unit should be a pace, but whose thumb, and whose pace? And suppose that the agreed-upon units don't integrate with each other very well—if there happened to be just over 37 standard thumbs in a standard pace, for example. The relative size of units would have to be modified so that they fitted together in socially and mathematically convenient ways.

All units of measurement are arbitrary, and could be different. Different units of length or distance existed in the past (cubits, leagues), and more recent "imperial" forms like feet and inches have been largely replaced by the international metric system. The metric system looks both logical and scientific because it is organized in tidy incremental units of ten, but its origin was arbitrary. The original definition of a meter was one ten-millionth of the distance from the equator to the North Pole on a line running through Paris—and was based on what turned out to be an inaccurate measurement. In 1983 the definition was changed to the distance traveled by light in a vacuum during 1/299,792,458 of a second, which is not something easily checked.

Catching Time by the Tail

The "second" to which I have referred (as the basis for legislating the exact length of a meter) is itself an arbitrary unit of *time*. The major units of time—day, month, year—are derived from astronomical phenomena, but the smaller units, like hours, minutes, and seconds, are human constructs.

It must always have seemed obvious to divide the passage of time into units corresponding to the interval between one sunrise and another (the apparent revolution of the sun around the earth), or one full moon and another (the apparent revolution of the moon round the earth), or the time that elapsed before the sun or a particular star returned to a particular part of the sky (the apparent revolution of the heavens around the earth). And each measure had an importance in its own right, for purposes of social organization, religious ritual, agriculture, navigation, and astronomy.[4]

But the cycles of natural phenomena don't combine neatly with each other mathematically. The number of days in a lunar month (roughly 29½), or in a year (roughly 365¼), is not a neat round figure, nor is the number of lunar months in the calendar year. To add to the complication, the actual time it takes the moon to complete one revolution around the earth, the earth to revolve on its own axis, or the earth to complete one revolution around the sun, all vary in their own erratic ways. They could never be used as a basis for the clock or calendar time by which we humans try to organize our lives.[5]

So our 365-day year (with 366-day exceptions) and 24-hour day are only rough approximations of natural phenomena, while our twelve 28-, 29-, 30-, or 31-day months and seven-day weeks are awkward and arbitrary divisions of the year. The day itself is artificially divided into 24 sixty-minute hours, each consisting of 60 sixty-second minutes, based on arbitrary laboratory standards, not on observable natural phenomena.

The arbitrariness of all the standards by which time is divided means that no one can work out logically what the different divisions might be or how they are related to each other. A different civilization (or a different individual) could divide years and days into quite different units—based on a metric system, for example.[6]

Because the reasons for administering time in the way we do are not self-evident, learners have no choice but to memorize facts and relationships that can't be understood (because there is nothing to understand). Reference to the clock in the hope of helping learners to understand the mathematics of hours, minutes, and seconds, or to the calendar for months, weeks, and days, can't be of help because it is necessary to understand the units and the mathematics in order to understand the clock and the calendar.

Once again, mathematical procedures that look simple and self-evident to those familiar with them turn out to be complex and opaque to those who are not.

Nevertheless, the packaging of time and space into tidy interrelated units has enormous value. (I was going to say "incalculable" value, but the advantage of the packaging is precisely that the units *are* calculable.) Once space has been divided into miles, yards, and inches (or kilometers, meters, and centimeters), and time divided into years, days, hours, and minutes, then there are units that can be counted. And this is only the beginning. When countable units are available, the full panoply of mathematics can be brought to bear for all manner of useful and reliable calculations.

Other Ingenious Measures

All standard units of measurement have to be comparable to some physical criterion in order to be conventionally agreed upon and transportable. My idea of an hour or a meter has to be the same as your idea of these units. An office of standards or of weights and measures is an important part of every national administration. These days the ultimate standard references for even the most familiar units, like the length of a meter in terms of the speed of light, involve the most esoteric definitions.

Weight[7] is an interesting kind of measure because we can sense it directly. By holding an object we can experience its "weight," and by comparing different objects we can sense which is the heavier. Weighing also can involve a delicate physical act, the balancing of objects on either side of a pivot point, or fulcrum. Establishing and comparing weights by hand and then by means of a balance must be one of the oldest technologies known to human beings, in both construction and commerce, even preceding mathematical calculation.

Conventional units of weight—and there have been many of them—were originally portable objects that had been balanced against some arbitrary criterion, like a fixed amount of water. When international standards were established, the prototypical kilogram was the weight of a metrical volume of pure water at a fixed temperature. This was an awkward standard to maintain, so it became a solid lump of metal that shared the same weight as the water. The current international standard is a solid piece of platinum-iridium alloy kept at a constant temperature in a laboratory in France, with other countries holding copies.

Weight originally was defined in terms of a fixed quantity of water, and temperature is defined in relation to the freezing and boiling points of water. The primary way we understand temperature is a combination of a bodily sensation (warmth, cold) and a number on a scale. But the familiar way in which temperature is measured is in terms of distance—the expansion or contraction of a column of a liquid metal (mercury) in a narrow glass tube.

A different kind of unit altogether is based on *angular* measurement—the familiar attribution of *degrees* to indicate the difference in direction in which two lines point. Angular measurement is established arbitrarily by slicing a circle into 360 equal pie-shaped parts, each of which is called a degree. Anyone can make this judgment exactly—in principle at least—so that no official unit of one degree need be kept in any national bureau of standards.

More precisely, a degree is the angular distance covered when a line from the center of a circle is turned 1/360 of the distance around the circumference; it is a unit of rotation.[8]

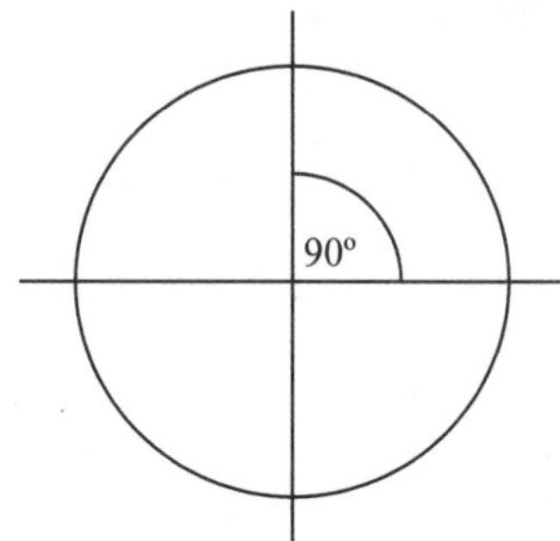

A straight line through the center of a circle from one side to the other produces two halves of 180 degrees each, and a vertical line from the horizontal or base line creates the familiar 90-degree right angle.

Right angles were widely known and employed in antiquity. They also can be constructed by folding a piece of paper in half twice, by forming a triangle with sides of particular lengths (with the ratio of 3, 4 and 5, for example), or by the use of two venerable carpenter's tools, a plumb bob formed by a pebble suspended on the end of a piece of string, and a spirit level, or simply a shallow open container of fluid.

Degrees are mathematically defined in terms of *movement* round the circumference of a circle. Rightward rotation of a vertical line from the center of a circle through a quarter of its circumference produces an angle of 90 degrees. Rotation through half the circumference is 180 degrees, and one complete circuit around the circle produces 360 degrees. The concept of rotation makes sense of negative angles (rotation in the opposite direction) and of angles of more than 360 degrees (more than one complete rotation). Some mathematicians feel that negative numbers, particularly their multiplication and division, are best understood in terms of rotation of the number sequence.

Technical units of measurement exist in every specialized field, for light, sound, smell, color, electricity, energy, power, and much else. The names of many of these units are encountered regularly in our daily lives without our necessarily understanding them—like calories, volts, and watts—and many others are used and understood only by experts.

Derived Measures

I have been using a variety of terms for the division of space—distance, length, breadth, height. They all refer to the same kind of measure, usually called linear (or distance in a line). They refer to extension in a flat plane in one dimension only. But many familiar mathematical units have been devised for two- and three-dimensional space, calculated from combinations of linear units, while more exotic units accommodate distances and directions in space that don't have flat surfaces at all.

The most familiar measure of two-dimensional space is *area*, calculated from linear distance in two directions, like length and width, or width and height. Small areas are expressed in such customary units as square inches, feet, and yards (or square centimeters and meters.) But larger units of area may have their own names, like *acres* (a typical imperial oddity consisting of 4840 square yards, the equivalent of 1⁄640 of a square mile) and *hectares* (10,000 square meters) for metric measure.

Square measurements don't necessarily refer to square areas. The areas of circles, triangles, and all other bounded forms are expressed in square measure.

Some two-dimensional measures are constructed from units of both space and time, for example, velocity, which computes changes in position over time, and acceleration, involving changes to velocity over time.

Three-dimensional units involve volume and commonly are expressed in cubic form—cubic inches and feet, or cubic centimeters and meters, all calculated by multiplying an area by a third linear distance. There are cubic measures of capacity that are particularly useful for materials that are not easy to count (like salt, sugar, corn, or liquids), including imperial pints and gallons and metric liters.

The huge diversity of systems of measurement that exists across the world demonstrates the ingenuity with which people in different communities at different times have striven to bring the detail of their daily lives under mathematical control. Much of the richness and color (and confusion and incompatibility) of these historical systems is being rationalized and standardized into metric form. But many of the traditional units survive.

Uniquely distinctive units are still used occasionally, for example, by pharmacists (grains, drams), cooks (spoons, cups), jewelers (carats), mariners (fathoms, knots), printers (points, picas), and surveyors (chains), and for paper (quires, reams), cloth (bolts), and wood (board feet, cords).

The possibilities for the expression and development of thought that the construction of distinctive units opens up do not end with mathematics. Anything that can be counted can be represented graphically—in point graphs, bar graphs, pie charts, and other visible forms—to show relationships among numbers and even solve numerical problems without mathematical calculation.

And reduction to the most elementary of units, to successions of zeroes and ones (or of presence and absence, or "open" and "shut") have made possible the "digitization" involved in many contemporary electronic technologies, including the high-fidelity reproduction of visual images and sound.

Measures That Elude

Despite the striking array of countable units that the human brain has devised in its endeavors to lay a mathematical net over the world, not everything we may be interested in is easily reduced to measurement. Many significant aspects of daily life continue to elude the unitizing zeal of counters and measurers.

Economics, sociology, and psychology, for example, have remained largely inexact sciences because of the difficulty of measuring anything involving human values, feelings, and emotions. What would a unit of joy, sadness, desire, deprivation, health, anger, fear, or loss be like?

Highly approximate and even arguable measures sometimes are employed so that human behavior can be subjected to statistical analysis, and often a reality is attributed to these measures that they do not warrant. This has especially been the case in education, where students are given equivocal "scores" and "grades" for various kinds of achievement. Students, parents, journalists, politicians, and educational authorities often take these dubious units seriously, comparing individuals and institutions with each other and making decisions that can have monumental effects on people's lives.

The belief that putting numbers to people's abilities and behavior is "objective" has the converse effect of downgrading human judgment. Experience and wisdom may count for nothing in the face of a few statistics, though the numbers may be far more approximate or biased than the judgments of people who understand situations from a broad perspective. Of course, human beings also can make decisions that are erratic and prejudiced, but it is often easier to detect and rectify such anomalies in people than it is in ironclad numbers.

CHAPTER 9

Notation—Signposts in the World of Mathematics

At the very least, mathematics is everything that can be done with numbers. Yet numbers alone can be used for little more than simple counting. Anything you want to do with numbers, any pattern or relationship you want to explore, requires *notation.* And notation is the rock on which many mathematical enterprises founder; the place where natural language and mathematics conspicuously part company on opposite sides of the glass wall. Even the ubiquitous = sign can never be fully explained in words.

For as long as people have had numbers, they have had to invent notation to make use of them. Yet many people who have problems with mathematics find notation more troublesome than numbers. How is it that something that is supposed to help becomes such a hindrance?

Let's try first to clarify what we are talking about or, at least, to clarify the language used in discussing mathematical notation. Once more we'll find that everyday language isn't entirely helpful when we talk about mathematical topics—that is one of the problems. But since everyday language is the only language we have for general communication, we'd better examine how precise it is when discussing the notation of mathematics.

The following are the kinds of mathematical notation I'm referring to:

+ − × (or * or •) ÷ (or /) =

together with the somewhat more esoteric:

( ) ∴ < > ± ≥ ∠ √ ∈ Σ ∫ ∪ ⊃ ⊇ π Δ and many others,

and some Greek counterparts:

α β Ψ χ ω

and, for that matter, the numbers themselves:

1 2 3 . . . (occasionally in Roman form: I II III . . .)

The dots . . . are also mathematical notation, indicating that the series could be continued.

What exactly are we dealing with in this rich array of notational devices? They are talked about in various ways. Sometimes they're called *signs* (as in "+ is the plus sign") and sometimes *symbols* (as in "+ and – are mathematical symbols"). Sometimes they are said to *indicate* certain mathematical states of affairs, and other times to *represent* them.

What are they, signs or symbols, indicators or representations? And does it make any difference what they are called? What else, if anything, should they be called?

To some extent, what they're called makes an obvious difference. Some people who feel little affinity for mathematics say it's because they have difficulty thinking symbolically, or that the sight of a symbol creates a mental block in them. But I've never met anyone who admitted a similar kind of trouble with signs. If the notational devices of mathematics were referred to as signs, rather than symbols, would the glass wall be removed?

Signs, Symbols, Icons, Indicators, and Representations

As usual, there's no point in consulting dictionaries to find out what exactly the words *sign* and *symbol* mean. Dictionaries tell us how particular words are used, but not what people who use those words really think they are talking about.

The problem is not that people use words imprecisely, but (as I've stated several times before) that words in unlegislated everyday language don't have precise meanings.

In one very common sense, a *sign* is simply an indication of what you may or should do—turn right, stop, don't smoke, pay here, exit, parking, tickets, fast food, and so on. In this sense, + and – might reasonably be considered signs; they indicate addition and subtraction. A sign commonly is considered to be arbitrary, without an obvious connection or resemblance to what it is supposed to indicate. It doesn't "stand for" anything, in the sense that it can take its place.

Some signs, however, may be prophetic and closely associated with what they indicate. Dark clouds are a sign of rain. Clenched fists are signs of anger. (Signs that are deliberately contrived to have a resemblance to what they are intended to represent, like the male and female signs on washroom doors and the multitude of tiny images on computer monitors, sometimes are also called *icons.*)

And in one very common sense, a *symbol* is simply something that stands for something else, usually with a conceptual association if not a direct resemblance. The crown is a symbol of royalty, the gun a symbol of power, the dove a symbol of peace. A corporate logo is a symbol. Symbols, in this sense, are tokens of what they stand for. They can be worshiped or feared. If you can't salute the king, you salute the flag.

But the word symbol also is commonly used to refer to a particular kind of typographical form—a "character" on a typewriter or computer keyboard. There's nothing symbolic about the symbols on my keyboard, though I certainly wouldn't call them signs.

There's no clear dividing line between the way the two words are used in everyday life. Things we might call signs on one occasion are called symbols on another.[1]

Sometimes we can't tell whether something is intended to be a sign, symbol, or icon in any sense unless we understand the thought behind it. An animal painted on a cave wall might be a *representation* of something the artist saw during the day, an *indication* of what was on someone's mind, a *sign* that a hunter had just made a kill, or a *symbol* of something to be worshiped.

There's nothing unusual in all of this. Similar ambiguity exists with musical notation. What is 𝄞? It is a sign when it indicates that a certain note or notes should be played or sung in the treble clef; it is a symbol when it is printed on the front cover of a concert program; and in company with a lot of other musical notation it represents a passage of music.

From a typographical point of view, all mathematical notation is symbols (without being symbolic). From a practical point of view, all mathematical notation is signs that something has been done, or should be done. But from a purely mathematical point of view, all notation represents relationships.[2]

Signs, symbols, icons, representations, and indicators (not to forget images, operators, emblems, and abstractions) are a cluster of words that cover a range of meanings, sometimes overlapping, and usually having more than one meaning each. The richness of use is typical of language—in fact, it contributes to the power of language—and is a problem only when people want to claim a particular precision in their use of words, or believe that close examination of a word will reveal an essential truth about whatever the word refers to. All everyday language use is conventional, depending largely on historical accident and implicit communal understanding and agreement.

So where does this leave us with mathematical notation? It means it doesn't matter how we talk about the various notational devices—whether we call them signs, symbols, marks, characters, or whatever—provided we don't think the names reveal anything profound about notation itself. And provided we don't think that there is something distinctive about mathematical notation that makes it intrinsically more difficult to understand than similar devices in other contexts.

And what, if anything, is the essential meaning or purpose behind different kinds of mathematical notation? One possibility, to which I have already alluded, is to simply say that notation is used to represent particular mathematical ideas or states of affairs. An alternative possibility, which carries a great deal of power, is to regard notation as an intermediary between the human mind and the world of mathematics.

THE ROLE OF MATHEMATICAL NOTATION

Let me introduce a new metaphor. Every time you do something mathematical—or think mathematically—you unroll in your mind part of an imaginary tapestry of limitless extent, every tiny stitch of which is a number. And each of these stitches is part of an endless series of intricate patterns.

If you follow the same stitches, you will discover the same patterns, the same relationships. And so will anyone else who follows the same route. There are innumerable patterns among these stitches, some familiar but many not yet revealed to most people, and others not yet discovered by anyone. You can follow directions to reveal patterns in which you are particularly interested, and you can leave directions so that others can uncover the same patterns.

The remarkable thing about this tapestry is that you do not have to unroll a substantial amount of it in order to explore a particular part. The numbers you will not be interested in, or that you will not require, do not need to be disturbed. To add or multiply 472 and 476, you do not need to think about 473, 474, 475, or any other number that is irrelevant to your particular purpose, nor need you think of subtraction, division, or square roots.

What enables you to make these precise and specific moves—for which fine needlework might well be the most appropriate analogy? Notation.

Notation indicates different kinds of pattern that can exist among the stitches of the magic tapestry of numbers. It doesn't indicate all possible kinds of pattern—nothing could—but it indicates particularly significant and useful ones. It also shows you how to uncover particular aspects of those patterns.

Notation is much like the cartographic symbols on a map, which link the human mind with the part of the physical world that the map represents. The notation of mathematics links the human mind with pathways and features of the world of mathematics. It helps us to understand what is behind the glass wall.

The Power of Equality

Perhaps the most important relationship in all of mathematics, throughout all its long and complex history, is the relationship represented by one of the first signs that every beginner learns, that of equality. I am talking of the = sign, the most important yet least discussed notational device of all.

Equality is the pivot on which every mathematical statement balances. Anyone who doesn't understand "equals" will never understand mathematics.

Yet the concept of equality is rarely taught specifically, and when it is, the explanation is probably approximate and incomplete. It has to be. Equality in mathematics is something that has to be understood from the inside, experienced rather than taught. Equality, mathematically speaking, can't be put into words, as I noted in Chapter 3.

Sometimes the = sign is seen as the link between a question and an answer; 2 + 3 is the question, and 5 is the answer. This is especially the case in primary grades in school, where every line of the mathematics exercises and drills is littered with = signs. At higher levels of mathematical reasoning, the = sign indicates successive steps in an argument or demonstration, where nothing may appear on the left:

$$\begin{aligned} \tfrac{1}{2} + \tfrac{3}{4} &= \tfrac{2}{4} + \tfrac{3}{4} \\ &= \tfrac{5}{4} \\ &= 1\tfrac{1}{4} \end{aligned}$$

The ladders of = signs can sometimes extend over pages of mathematical reasoning, without anything ever appearing on the left of the sign after the first line. It is hardly adequate to say that each = indicates equality with the line above. Rather, each = represents another step in a complex yet directed sequence of moves from the first statement on the left of the sign to the final statement on the right. Each = , in other words, indicates a slight change of direction in a progression from one mathematical pattern to another, a movement from one stitch to another.

Each step may be an equality, but the entire sequence is a journey. Every = introduces a movement that has a purpose because it leads from one point—the starting point—to a destination that may be far distant. The destination may be familiar (a demonstration) or hitherto unknown (a discovery), and the journey from starting point to destination might be accomplished in other ways (as it is in mathematical "proofs"). But every = is a guarantee that the trail was followed without any breaks in the path, that the mathematical thread was unbroken.

By now, of course, I am awash in metaphor. But every attempt to explain = in everyday language is doomed to be metaphorical. The = sign has a meaning, a very precise meaning, but it is a meaning that can never be fully explained in words; it can only be intuited and understood mathematically. In one sense, 1 + 1 = 2 explains everything about the = sign.

Signs Familiar and Unfamiliar

Because the +, –, ×, and ÷ signs are familiar, we tend to think they are both obvious and straightforward. Though commonly referred to as operators, or as signs for mathematical "operations," these signs are in fact expressions of relationships; they represent particular relationships among the endless patterns of numbers, the way musical notation represents different kinds of melody, rhythm, and harmony.

By themselves, 472 and 473 indicate nothing, but linked by the familiar +, – , ×, and ÷ signs, they form unique pathways among the endless patterns of numbers.

So do other notational devices, which for many people may be less familiar, such as those for squared numbers ($3^2 = 9$) and for square roots ($\sqrt{9} = 3$). A notation that delighted me on first acquaintance is the factorial sign, or !, which succinctly indicates (with evident surprise) a number multiplied by every whole number lower than itself:

$$6! = 6 \times 5 \times 4 \times 3 \times 2 \times 1 = 720$$

A small superscripted circle, of course, indicates that we are in the realm of degrees, as in 90°. To represent angles by a small zero might be considered odd, but no more so than the notation for fractions of a degree, one-sixtieth part being a *minute*, represented as ’ , and a sixtieth of which is a *second*, represented by ” . Minutes and seconds are also of course subdivisions of an hour, to the same sixtieth proportions, and they are represented by the same ’ and ” signs.

Surprisingly, given that mathematics arises from the basic "more than" and "less than" relationship so familiar to everyone, including children, the mathematical notation for "more than" and "less than" (> and <) is introduced relatively late in many people's mathematical development, and often causes some bewilderment.

The relationships represented by > and < may be particularly difficult to comprehend when used in such expressions as

$$20 < X < 30$$

which is supposed to be read as "20 is less than the number represented by X, which is less than 30."

A more comprehensible way of making that same statement might be "X is a number between 20 and 30," or "X is more than 20 and less than 30." In both cases, X is the subject of the expression and is most comprehensibly read first. But neither "X > 20, X < 30" nor "X > 20 < 30" is a grammatical mathematical statement. The expression "20 < X < 30" makes sense only from a mathematical perspective, not as a sentence to be read off one element at a time.

Some notational devices are employed specifically to help readers find their way around mathematical expressions, and to ensure that wrong turns aren't taken. These signs, when and if they are used, follow very strict rules, the first being that they always appear in pairs. I am referring to *braces* (or brackets) like ( ), { }, and [ ].

Sometimes braces are used optionally, simply for the sake of clarity, as I occasionally write the more legible (5 × 2) rather than 5 × 2 in this text. Sometimes they are obligatory. Often they are nested, as in expressions like $(33 \div (7 + 6(12 - 7)))$, where the computation indicated by the innermost pair of braces must always be done first. The preceding expression is regarded as perfectly good mathematical form, despite the piling up of braces on the right. But nested parentheses are rarely acceptable in written language—(where they would be regarded as clumsy (and confusing (to many people)))—and would never be read from the inside out.

WHEN X MARKS THE SPOT

For the first time, in the last few pages, I have introduced the ubiquitous letter X to take the place of unknown or specific numbers. It is time to refer to those occasions when mathematical symbols really are symbols, because they stand for something else. (I'll use the capital X for legibility and contrast, but in mathematics it is just as likely to turn up in lower case, while in some contexts x, y, z and X, Y, Z have different functions or meanings.)

The use of letters to take the place of numbers has a history and name, *algebra*,[3] that go back to antiquity, and has added immense power to mathematics. In effect, it enables mathematicians to study what numbers do without actually using numbers.

In mathematical expressions, the familiar A, B, C and X, Y, Z stand for any number. Sometimes you're told what that number is, as in X = 7, and sometimes you're not. Sometimes you must work out or find out what X represents: 5 + X = 7, therefore X = 2. In such cases, X is referred to as an *unknown*. But at other times there is no specific number that the letter represents, and it is referred to as a *variable*. The particular number that variable X represents on any occasion depends on the context that X is in; on the part of the mathematical pattern you are looking at. It's a chameleon of a number. Children typically have no trouble when they encounter X as an unknown, but can be confused by X as a variable.

The use of letters as variables can circumvent a great deal of mathematical repetition. The practical ancient recipe for constructing a right-angled triangle was to make sides in the proportion 3, 4, and 5, because all triangles are right-angled if the squares of the two shorter sides together equal the square of the longest side. (For example, $3^2 + 4^2 = 5^2$, that is, 9 + 16 = 25.) But there are many other ways of constructing a right angle; one of them is $9^2 + 12^2 = 15^2$, that is, 81 + 144 = 225. A simple way to express all such relationships is that a right-angled triangle is produced when the three sides, labeled a, b, and c, have the relationship $a^2 + b^2 = c^2$.

There are also occasions when a particular number isn't known and we'd like to use a "place-holder" so that we can get on with our mathematical business. An algebraic symbol is used in the same way that we might put a bookmark into a book to indicate the location of something we don't at the moment understand, but want to return to when we have discovered the meaning.

Algebraic formulas can be used by specialists in many professions to solve complex equations, and algebra is employed by a few specialized mathematicians to explore mathematics itself, making it almost the language of mathematics. It is easier to express the structures of the number system with algebra, just as it is easier to say things about people in general if we don't try to list all their individual names.

Heart of Darkness

Many people have difficulty with algebra—even with a single algebraic symbol—or any other kind of mathematical notation. They explain that they "can't think symbolically," or that they are made queasy just by the sight of symbols. They are blind to anything that isn't a letter or number in a familiar "real-world" context.

But it is hard to see why anyone should be afflicted in this way. "Symbol" is only a word (though it is perhaps the word that people who claim to dislike symbols are afraid of). We encounter symbols every day of our lives, and make sense of them, without being aware that we are doing so.

We understand icons on our computer screens. We have no difficulty with the meaning of ♂ and ♀. We have no problem regarding a flag as a symbol of a country, a ring as a symbol of commitment, or a stylized heart as a symbol of love. So why the difficulty with the inoffensive X, Y, and Zs? The only time people say they are afraid of symbols is when the subject is mathematics or some other "technical" subject.

A dread of symbols could be rationalization of a more general failure of understanding, or a relic of some particularly miserable experiences. But I suspect the underlying problem is that the victims of symbolophobia never get inside the world of mathematics to look at the notational devices from the inside. That is the heart of the problem. Lack of understanding invariably leads to difficulties with memorization.

From outside the world of mathematics, peering through the glass wall, people may well see mathematical symbols as ugly and indecipherable. Most people come to algebraic symbols a little later than to numbers; symbols are introduced as something different from numbers, and they look totally different from numbers. Just when we think the whole business of 1, 2, 3 . . . is safely under control, here come other symbols, some of which we also may be familiar with, like letters of the alphabet, but in a totally alien context. And as always, verbal explanations explain nothing to the mathematically uninitiated. Understanding has to be drawn out, not thrust in.

Not the End of the Story

All mathematical signs are arbitrary. They could all be different, and they often were different in the past. For Newton, less than 400 years ago, multiplication was indicated by putting the two numbers involved close to each other, with no specific sign at all.[4]

Mathematical signs are always subject to change, and we've by no means achieved the last word with the set we currently have.

Computers have brought about a good deal of change to mathematical notation, much of it simply to suit their own keyboards. The ÷ that was a staple of my own childhood is not (to my considerable inconvenience in this book) represented on my own keyboard, and has been widely replaced by the "slash" (/), which doesn't have very much else to do in person-to-person communication. The letter X on my keyboard is unsuited to be employed as the mathematical ×, and multiplication today is widely represented by the star or asterisk (*), another otherwise underemployed typographical symbol on the keyboard. Squaring a number is indicated by a double asterisk: 3** = 9. Even more obscurely, powers (self-multiples) of numbers are indicated by a caret: 3^2 = 9 ; 4^3 = 64 , which is also the notation employed on the calculator that I use.

Because of the arbitrariness of mathematical notation, there is no way that the meaning of mathematical signs can easily leap to the eye or mind of a learner, although people familiar with their use get the feeling that their meaning is obvious, unarguable, and immediate. What else could + mean but "plus"?[5]

CHAPTER 10

Numbers Between Numbers

Let's go further behind the glass wall, into the labyrinthine world of mathematics. The integers (the positive and negative whole numbers) have limitless possibilities for constructing new numbers. Add any two numbers, no matter how big, and there will always be a number that is the exact total. Multiply any two numbers, no matter how big, and a number will be found that is the precise product of the other two numbers.

The same limitless possibilities apply with subtraction, provided that we make use of 0 and all the "negative" numbers. Negative numbers also ensure that a precise result can always be found for the addition, multiplication, and subtraction of numbers smaller than 0. It may not be easy to imagine circumstances in which we might want to multiply such small numbers, especially as the result is an even smaller number, but it is comforting to know that no matter how large or small the numbers we are dealing with, there is no risk that we will ever run out of numbers for addition, subtraction, and multiplication.

But the system of whole numbers also has innumerable gaps. While integers can always be relied upon to provide a needed value for addition, multiplication, and subtraction, a whole number can't always be found for division. If you try to divide 3 by 2, or 8 by 3, the value is something that falls between two adjacent whole numbers. It is more than one number but less than the next.

For early explorers of the world of mathematics, the need to fill the spaces between integers was an awkward problem. But again the number system demonstrated its remarkable versatility. Miniature number systems could be created to fill the cracks between whole numbers, worlds within worlds, while integrating themselves seamlessly into the larger system. One familiar way to construct such subsystems was through fractions.

FRACTIONS

It took the human race hundreds of years to work out that fractions could fill the spaces between whole numbers, and many people today find difficulty in understanding or using them. Many children have difficulty understanding that fractions are *numbers* and can be treated in exactly the same ways as whole numbers. Fractions are not intuitively obvious.

Ask people whether they understand fractions, and they may say "of course" and talk of dividing pies or pizzas into a small number of slices. But this doesn't mean they understand the mathematics of fractions; they understand cutting up pies. They have scarcely ventured beyond everyday language and everyday experience. Some people even claim to understand fractions because they can remember a rule or two, for example, that to divide one fraction by another you invert the second fraction and multiply ($1/2 \div 1/3 = 1/2 \times 3/1 = 1\frac{1}{2}$). But they can't say *why* this should be the case, or even give an estimate of what the result might be.

I'm not saying that any of this is due to ignorance or lack of application to instruction. It's because the person hasn't entered the world of mathematics. Further dedicated practice might improve the "skill" of doing routine mathematical problems with fractions, but it wouldn't improve understanding. That's because much of the thinking that fractions demand is contrary to everyday reasoning. Fractions are impossible to understand from the "real-world" side of the glass wall. It's one thing to visualize relationships among a few slices of a pie, and another matter altogether to contemplate the relationships of fractions to each other and to whole numbers in the world of mathematics.

The Nature of Fractions

The idea that something might be complete in itself yet a functioning part of something much larger is not an alien concept outside mathematics. The distinction between a part and a whole is fundamental to the way infants instinctively organize their experience, and is reflected in every language.

Expressions like "part of," "piece of," and "some of" are commonly used and understood by people with no mathematical knowledge at all. The same applies to the more specific term "half, " and possibly also to "quarter." But other words for fractions are taken directly from mathematics, like "fifth," "sixth," and "seventh," and can only be understood mathematically. It is difficult to imagine a fifth or seventh equal part of a pizza, and impossible to imagine a fifteenth or seventeenth part, or the difference between them.

People in the distant past probably talked about "halves" long before they knew anything of mathematics, and the same is true for small children and other nonmathematical people today. But everyday language and experience do little to assist understanding of the complexities that surround fractions in mathematical contexts. The status and functions of fractions were an enigma to experienced mathematicians for hundreds of years. Students are expected to learn about them, but they're usually not told why, or what mathematical problems fractions are supposed to solve.

Two distinct problems were encountered as people in the past tried to find ways of making sense of the pieces left over after one number was divided by another, pieces that were never encountered or required in the addition, subtraction, and multiplication of integers. One specific problem was to find a way to think about *parts* of whole numbers—to have a concept of what $\frac{1}{3}$ or $\frac{5}{7}$ might mean, beyond something less than a whole number. The second, more general problem was to find a systematic way to fill in the spaces between all integers with parts that themselves had the mathematical properties of numbers.

Making Sense of Fractions

What is the one third or two thirds ($\frac{1}{3}$ or $\frac{2}{3}$) that might be left over (the "remainder") from a division like $7 \div 3$ or $8 \div 3$? The clarifying realization that gradually dawned was that the problem was its own answer. Nothing had to be done with the $\frac{1}{3}$ or $\frac{2}{3}$; they just had to be looked at differently. The solution is a mathematical sleight of hand.

What is one divided by three? A third. One divided by three is the equivalent of a one-third part, or $\frac{1}{3}$. What is two divided by three? Two thirds—two divided by three is the equivalent of two one-third parts, or $\frac{2}{3}$.

The question and the answer happen to sound and look the same, but they mean different things because they are produced from a different point of view for a different purpose. It is like one person asking, "Great vacation?" to acquire some information, and the other responding, "Great vacation!" to provide that information.

Even the mathematical notation came to reflect the similarity that bridged the difference. For clarity in books, and in working with beginners, division usually is indicated by the ÷ sign, as in $2 \div 3$. The same problem also can be depicted with one number placed above the other, as in $\frac{2}{3}$. But an alternative more generally employed by experienced users of mathematics is to keep everything on one line, indicating the division by a slash /. Thus $2 \div 3$ also can be written 2/3.

Fractions customarily are also written one over the other, as in $\frac{2}{3}$, especially for beginners. But once again they can be written on one line with the slash /, as in 2/3 for two thirds.

So we have the odd situation that a division and its result can be written in the following repetitious form:

$$2/3 = 2/3$$

This is not as redundant and meaningless as it looks. To read "2/3 = 2/3" correctly you have to say something like "two divided by three is two thirds." The same digits on the two sides have different names. The 2 on the left (in the division "problem") is called the *dividend* (the number to be divided) and the 3 next to it is the *divisor* (the number the dividend is to be divided by). The 2 on the right (in the fractional solution) is called the *numerator* (it enumerates the number of parts you have) and the 3 next to it is the *denominator* (it denominates the magnitude of those parts).

There is another critical mathematical difference. The "division" on the left expresses a particular relationship between two independent numbers, the 2 and the 3. The fraction on the right is a number in its own right. Every fraction (like ⅓, ⅔, 5/7, and 17/82) may look like a combination of numbers, but in fact it can—and must—be treated as a single quantity. When fractions are added to the group of *natural numbers* (1, 2, 3 . . .), expanded by zero and negatives into *integers* (. . . -3, -2, -1, 0, 1, 2, 3 . . .), the entire collection is mathematically referred to as the *rational numbers*, the word rational indicating that they are all considered numbers in the face of reason.

So what is it that the two sides of the equation, the problem and the solution, have in common? Why should they look the same yet have different roles?

The answer is that they both express a *ratio*—the same ratio—from different points of view. The "problem" of 1 ÷ 3 (divide one by three) can be interpreted to mean "find a number that has the same proportion to one as one has to three. The fractional "solution" ⅓ is a number that has the same proportion to one as one has to three.

The problem 2 ÷ 3 requires finding a number that has the same proportion to 2 as 2 has to 3. The fraction ⅔ is a number that has the same proportion to 2 as 2 has to 3.

Ratios

A number is complete in itself. It is 3 or 5 or 8, just as an animal is a horse, a cow, or a tiger (or something else). You don't have to say, for a number or for an animal, that what it is depends on the company that it's keeping. Numbers are *pure* magnitudes. Even fractions are pure magnitudes.

A ratio, on the other hand, is a *relative* magnitude; it is a *proportion* involving two numbers. Just as a horse can't be regarded as large or small unless you compare it with another horse, so a ratio can exist only when one number is compared with another.

The ratio of 2 to 3 (written 2 : 3), for example, is the proportion of the number 2 compared with the number 3, or of 2 of something with 3 of something else. It sounds perhaps redundant to say that the numbers 2 and 3 stand in the ratio of 2 to 3 to each other, but so do 4 and 6, 20 and 30, 40 and 60, and innumerable other pairs of numbers that can be reduced to a proportionate relationship of 2 : 3.

Two cups of flour to three cups of sugar is a ratio of 2 : 3. So is 20 cups of flour to 30 cups of sugar. Or 6 bags of sand to 9 bags of cement.

In other words, a ratio is a fixed relationship between two numbers. It can be applied to any number, and to anything that numbers can be applied to. Given the ratio and one number, the other number can be determined. If the ratio is 5 : 4 and the number on the left is 15, the other number must be 12. If the ratio is 5 : 4 and the number on the right is 16, then the number on the left must be 20.

Ratios normally aren't numbers—they are relationships between two numbers. Being told that you must mix flour and sugar to the ratio of 2 : 3 doesn't tell you how much flour and sugar you need. But when ratios are used as fractions—when you want to specify a point in the number sequence that exists two thirds of the way between 7 and 8, or between 53 and 54, then $2/3$ *is* a number. *In other words, a fraction is a ratio regarded as a number.*

Fractions can be treated like all other numbers. They can be put in order (like $1/4$, $1/3$, $1/2$, or the more complicated sequence $1/4$, $3/11$, $1/3$, $5/12$, $1/2$). Like all other numbers, fractions can be added, subtracted, multiplied, and divided, with each other or with whole numbers (with a few important exceptions mainly involving 0).[1] The orderly flexibility of fractions within the entire number system is another remarkable aspect of the simple basic technology of counting, systematically putting one thing after another.

So far I have been talking about what are called "proper fractions," or fractions that are smaller than one (the distance between one whole number and the next). Numbers larger than one can be written in fractional (or ratio) form, for example, $4/3$ or $231/16$. Fractions that are larger than (or equal to) one are referred to as "improper" fractions. They can always be "reduced" to whole numbers and their fractional parts, $4/3$ becoming $1\,1/3$, and $231/16$ becoming $14\,7/16$, while $64/16$ is simply $4/1$, which is of course 4.

To sum up, a fraction is a ratio or proportion of the numerical distance between one number and the next. By itself, $1/7$ is one-seventh part of the numerical distance between 0 and 1. The number $4\,1/7$ is four plus one-seventh part of the numerical distance between 4 and 5.

Language and Other Conceptual Problems

It is not always easy to see how fractions function as individual numbers. This is partly because of problems with language, but also because of conceptual complexities in dealing with fractional quantities. In the following examples we'll consider only positive fractions, which are complicated enough. But anything that can be done with negative whole numbers also can be done with negative fractions, sometimes with consequences so Byzantine (except from a mathematical point of view) that I shall avoid any reference to them.

The addition of fractions is not difficult to understand, even though it might be complicated to carry out. Add two or more fractions together and you get a bigger fraction, as you *can* demonstrate with portions of a cake. And a fraction gets smaller if you subtract a fraction, which similarly can be related to our everyday experience of the world.

But multiplication is a problem. We normally expect things to get bigger when they are multiplied. Two multiplied by two is four, a larger number. But a half times a half is a quarter ($\frac{1}{2} \times \frac{1}{2} = \frac{1}{4}$), a smaller amount.

Division by fractions is perhaps worse. A fraction divided by another fraction results in a larger number. We don't normally expect things that are divided to get bigger. The logic may seem reasonable that there are two quarters in a half—but the division of a half by a quarter ($\frac{1}{2} \div \frac{1}{4} = 2$) defies everything but the mathematical imagination.

Simple division with whole numbers, like $4 \div 2 = 2$, often is expressed in something like the following form: "Divide four candies between 2 children—and each gets two." But if you divide half a candy bar by a half—if that were possible—the result would be a whole candy bar.

Many people can see that whole numbers divided by themselves always result in a value of 1: $2 \div 2 = 1$; $14 \div 14 = 1$; $82 \div 82 = 1$. But this understanding is not easily extended to numbers that are smaller than 1. It is not immediately obvious that $\frac{1}{2} \div \frac{1}{2} = 1$, that $\frac{1}{4} \div \frac{1}{4} = 1$, or that $\frac{1}{82} \div \frac{1}{82} = 1$. This makes sense on the mathematical side of the glass wall, but nowhere else.

Small wonder that many people never fully understand the "operations" involved in the multiplication and division of fractions. They may learn the rituals for long enough to get through examinations, but what doesn't make sense to them is rarely retained for any length of time. What is the point of remembering something that is seemingly nonsense?

It is not that such people have learned nothing at school, but they have learned the wrong thing. They have learned to expect that multiplication makes something bigger and that division makes it smaller. They have learned this from innumerable classroom explanations and demonstrations. And it all seems intuitively obvious—until they have a need or desire to think mathematically.

Although fractions are numbers, there are two major differences between the whole number system and the subsidiaries that plug the gaps. The first difference is that the distance from one whole number to the next is fixed: It is "one." The distance between any two adjacent whole numbers, such as 5 and 6, or 595 and 596, is always one, and it is always obvious which of two numbers, adjacent or not, is bigger. The distance between two adjacent fractions is variable, however. It has to be calculated. The distance between $^2/_5$ and $^3/_5$ is $^1/_5$. The distance between $^2/_{23}$ and $^3/_{23}$ is $^1/_{23}$, which is much less than the distance between $^2/_5$ and $^3/_5$.

The second major difference between whole number systems and fractions is that while there is no end to the range of whole numbers available to us, fractions aren't homogenous the way integers are. If we are dealing with thirds, there are three of them between any two adjacent whole numbers, no more and no less. If we are dealing with sevenths, then seven is the limit. In effect we make an arbitrary decision to divide up the space between adjacent whole numbers into a fixed number of parts, and that is the total we must work with. Fractions lead a cramped existence.

It is impossible to talk about most fractions, or even to think about them, with anything like the facility with which we can handle whole numbers. It is usually not hard to understand that $^1/_2$ is bigger than $^1/_3$, even though 2 is not bigger than 3. This *can* be done with pies. But it is much more difficult to think about fractions like $^4/_5$ and $^7/_9$. You can't immediately see which of the two is bigger, the way you can see that 9 is bigger than 7.

Finally, there is the chasm between natural and mathematical language. The word "fraction" is rarely used in everyday language, and with nothing like its mathematical meaning. We might refer to a "fraction" of a pie instead of the more usual "piece" or "slice," but only when the piece is relatively small. In mathematics a fraction can be almost as large as the whole, like $^9/_{10}$ or $^{99}/_{100}$. Anyone who took three quarters of a pie and then claimed it was "only a fraction" would surely get an argument.

DECIMAL FRACTIONS

We haven't quite done with the complexities of fractions. One particular kind of fraction is singled out for special treatment in mathematics, and is familiar to all of us in a disguised form. And that is a fraction whose denominator is 10 or a multiple of 10.

Not only are fractions like $^1/_{10}$ and $^1/_{100}$ used for many special purposes, but their appearance is radically changed. The fraction $^1/_{10}$ is rewritten as 0.1; and

$\frac{1}{100}$ is rewritten as 0.01. The alternative forms are familiarly known as "decimals," of course. More formally they are "decimal fractions," a term that reveals their heritage.

The change from the $\frac{1}{10}$ to the 0.1 format permits a whole new dimension to be introduced into the world of numbers. Nevertheless, it all fits into the general pattern of fractional mathematics, filling in the gaps between whole numbers.

Segmenting Whole Numbers into Tenths

Decimal fractions are fractions that don't look like fractions because part of them is suppressed. You have to know there is a denominator, missing but understood.

Decimal fractions are represented by single numbers like 0.5, 0.25, and 0.05 rather than the equivalent pairs of numbers $\frac{5}{10}$, $\frac{25}{100}$, and $\frac{5}{100}$.

Decimal fractions always consist of two parts, separated (in some parts of the world) by a period, called the *decimal point.* (In other parts of the world, the decimal point may be a comma.) The number to the left of the decimal point is always an integer, like 4.567 or 0.123. The zero doesn't stand for anything (except itself), but it makes clear the function of the decimal point and helps line up numbers for computation.

The number to the right of the decimal point is the fractional part. Paradoxically, the value of the digits to the right of the decimal point varies with how many of them there are. In the decimal fraction 0.5, the five stands for five tenths. In the decimal fraction 0.05, the 5 stands for five hundredths, and in 0.005, the fraction stands for five thousandths. The decimal fraction 0.555 stands for five hundred and fifty five thousandths—$\frac{555}{1000}$.

The lower line of decimal fractions, the denominator, is always taken for granted. And unlike other fractions, which can have any number other than 0 as a denominator, the denominator of a decimal must always be a power of 10. (That is why they are *decimal* fractions.) The missing bottom line of a decimal fraction is always understood to be 10 to a power one more (to "one more place") than the number of digits in the part of the decimal fraction to the right of the decimal point. Thus 0.5 is understood to be equivalent to $\frac{5}{10}$, 0.25 is understood to be equivalent to $\frac{25}{100}$, and 0.005 is understood to be equivalent to $\frac{5}{1000}$.

Just like other fractions, decimal fractions are ratios—with the right side missing but understood. At any time the missing denominator can be replaced and if necessary simplified to show that decimal fractions and other fractions can both express the same ratio:

decimal fraction		understood fraction		ratio		simplified ratio		fraction
0.5	=	5⁄10	=	5 : 10	=	1 : 2	=	½
0.25	=	25⁄100	=	25 : 100	=	1 : 4	=	¼
0.005	=	5⁄1000	=	5 : 1000	=	1 : 200	=	1⁄200

Decimal fractions settle themselves easily and in an orderly manner into the spaces between whole numbers. Like nesting dolls, embedded within each tenth (one decimal place) can be found ten parts, or hundredths (two decimal places), within which can be found another ten parts, or thousandths (three decimal places), and so on, without end.

This is a third dimension of counting. The natural numbers climb endlessly upwards, one upon one upon one. Negative numbers pivot on zero to extend the natural numbers—now all called integers—in the opposite direction. And now decimals extend the same number system into finer and finer particles.

Decimal fractions can be added, subtracted, multiplied, and divided, with other decimal fractions and with whole numbers. They can be put into ascending and descending order far more easily than other fractions. There is nothing remotely similar to this versatility in language.

Missing Decimal Fractions

But there is always a catch. There are many fractions that can't be converted to decimal fractions (because a common denominator can't be found). Decimal 0.5 is identical with ½; decimal 0.25 is identical with ¼. But there is no exact decimal equivalent for ⅓.

From a decimal perspective a third is 0.333 . . . (3⁄10 plus 3⁄100 plus 3⁄1000 . . .), with the 3 endlessly repeated. Not surprisingly, this is termed a *repeating* decimal fraction.

The problem occurs with all proper fractions that don't have a denominator (the bottom line) that will divide without a remainder into 10 or a power of 10, which means 3, 7, and 9 and all other numbers ending in 1, 3, 7, or 9. There are just no nonrepeating decimal fractions available for them. Some decimal fractions get in to a loop and repeat whole blocks of digits, for example 1⁄7 = 0.142857142857142857 . . .

There are other occasions when no fractions at all, decimal or otherwise, can be found. Two ancient mathematical problems can never be solved with absolute exactitude because neither a whole number nor a nonterminating fraction can express the answer. I refer to the impossibility of finding an exact numerical value for the ratio of the diameter of a circle to its circumference, or for the ratio of the sides of a square to its diagonal.[2]

Playing the Percentages

There is one form of decimal fraction that is ubiquitous in our lives but rarely recognized for what it is. *Percentages* have seeped under the glass wall from mathematics into our daily language, and are used with far less precision than mathematics normally would demand.

Percentages even have their own special sign, % (note the zeroes again), which represents nothing mathematically but merely indicates that the number that precedes it is an abbreviated form of decimal fraction. Five percent (5%) means five one-hundredths of whatever is being discussed, and normally (mathematically) would be written 0.05. Ten percent (10%) is ten one-hundredths, or 0.1. Fifty percent (50%) is $^{50}/_{100}$, or a half.

Sometimes percentages are employed with relative precision—47 percent of the population voted in the last election; 32 percent of Belgians are native speakers of French. At other times the term is used quite loosely—the bookmaker keeps a percentage of the betting money; only a percentage of donations goes to the charity. Percentage, in these cases, simply means a part; it could be a large part or a small part. This is natural language, not mathematics.

Many people don't know what a percentage means mathematically. They might believe that any percentage (like any "fraction") has to be negligible. They don't understand that any calculation involving percentages requires conversion to fractional or decimal format.

CHAPTER 11

Numbers in Space

The word *geometry* means measurement of the earth—but very little geometry is actually done on the earth. Most geometry is done on paper (or on chalkboards or computer monitors) with abstract *representations* of the earth or selected portions of it. Learners usually are introduced to geometry on paper, as illustrations in books and in exercises. When we explore the world geometrically, we put the world on paper—or into our minds—in diagrammatic form.

Arithmetic is done on paper too, but this is calculation, not representation. The marks on the paper in calculation bear only a numerical resemblance to whatever is being calculated; they may tell you nothing about the size, shape, orientation, or quantity of whatever it is you are mathematically concerned with. But geometry is different.

Geometry occasionally is done on site, at first hand. Direct measurement of the dimensions and angles of a field, a building, or a piece of carpentry, is sometimes a practical way of making working calculations and decisions. Surveyors and mariners may take bearings directly from the landmarks or astronomical bodies with which they are concerned. But direct observation is often inconvenient and sometimes impossible. Geometry usually doesn't deal with physical reality, but with idealized or abstract representations of it. It deals with space.

The transfer of geometry from the earth to paper, or some other flat surface, permitted mathematicians to study the properties of geometrical forms. Geometricians were no longer studying the earth, or the heavens; they were studying geometry itself. All of Euclid's celebrated "theorems" of geometry—after 2300 years still regarded as worthy of study by high school students and by professional mathematicians—are based on the examination of forms on paper, "proved" by reason rather than by appeals to nature.

Until about 400 years ago, geometry was always something that made sense by eye. Geometry still has to make sense by eye for beginners, and this is often far from easy. In fact, whether geometry makes sense or not depends on the point of view.

A Matter of Perspective

The abstract nature of geometrical diagrams frequently causes early problems of understanding. Geometrical figures usually don't look much like whatever they are supposed to represent, and even when there is a resemblance, it is from a most unusual point of view. The world from a geometrical point of view is quite different from the way we usually perceive it.

The problem is not that scaled down and simplified outlines of objects are difficult to recognize. Children have no trouble seeing that

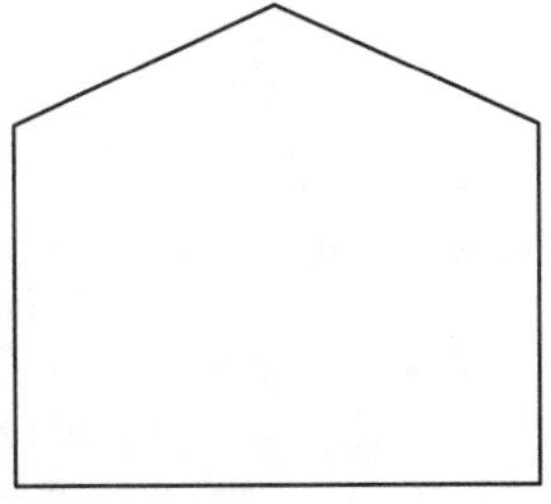
Figure 11.1

represents a house. They have no trouble even in seeing that a rectangle

Figure 11.2

could be a house, especially if a rudimentary door or window is included. (After all, children have no difficulty imagining that a wooden block they are playing with is a house, a table, or an automobile.)

But children—and many adults—encounter difficulty when told that the same shape

Figure 11.3

represents the *floor plan* of a house, or of a room, or that it represents a car park or a field. The difficulty is not the representation, it's the view.

You don't (unless you are in an aircraft) see fields and other terrestrial features from above. You don't see floors from directly overhead. Children don't have trouble with drawings, even very schematic ones, but they do have trouble with unusual points of view. We all do. Map reading demands training and experience. Fliers don't see islands the way mariners do. We prefer to see representations of the world the way we see the world itself, the way our eyes are located in our head—looking out toward the horizon. Geometry doesn't often offer us this.

There's another unnatural fact about the geometrical (and map-reading) point of view. It dispenses with perspective, which is not something that human eyes and brain are accustomed to.

Perspective is not something that geometry deliberately ignores; it is impossible for geometrical representations to include it (though perspective can be calculated geometrically). Geometry can represent one- or two-dimensional figures without difficulty, as in the preceding diagrams of a house. But it cannot represent three-dimensional objects in a single figure at all (unless distortion is part of the geometrical figure). The following drawing of a cube has geometrical distortions on two sides:

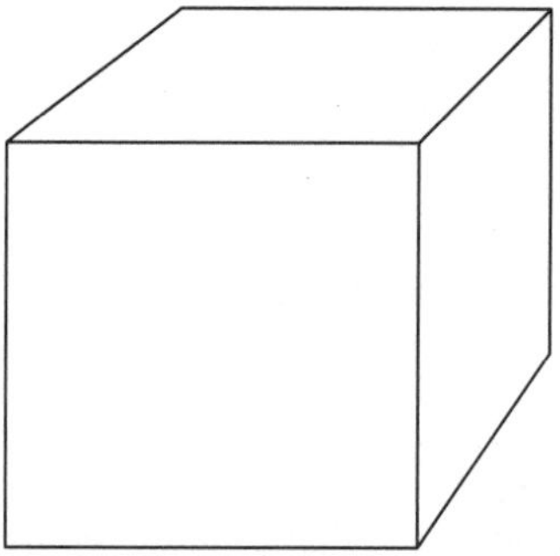

Figure 11.4

Neither the top nor the side of Figure 11.4 is an accurate geometrical representation of the square face of a cube.

The situation is further complicated because geometry is not actually concerned with solid substance, of objects or of portions of the earth, whether real or imagined. Geometry is concerned solely with *space*. And ironically, we can't *see* space, either in reality or in a geometrical diagram. So artificial lines have to be put around geometrical space, though the lines have no physical or mathematical reality.

Figure 11.5

When we are told that Figure 11.5 represents a field, the field is not the four lines, but the space within them. The lines themselves don't represent any physical or geometrical reality, but rather the space between the corners of the field. (Even if the field is surrounded by a fence, the lines of the geometrical representation represent the abstract perimeter along which the fence is assumed to lie, not the fence itself.) The distance between one landmark and another, in a map or a geometrical diagram, is not substantial at all—it is space. The angular difference between two compass points is a measurement of the slice of space between the two points.

For purely geometrical problems, involving triangles, circles, and other bounded shapes, the concern is always with space, whether it is the distance from one point to another, the various directions that the distances between points might take, or the angles between them. The lines that are drawn on a geometrical figure are there merely to delineate (literally) the boundaries and other characteristics of a chunk of space.

We are left with the odd situation that the way we normally see the world is not the way we encounter representations of it in geometry, and the geometrical view is not something we usually encounter in the world around us. We find, once more, that mathematical structures can be understood only from inside mathematics. The only way to understand geometrical figures is from the point of view of the figures themselves, with a geometrician's eyes.

Geometry and Maps

It shouldn't be surprising that the development of geometry in human history has been closely paralleled by the development of maps. Both geometry and maps involve the same conceptual challenge—to see the world, or part of the world, from what David Olson termed "the view from nowhere" (1994, p. 201).[1] In fact, it is sometimes difficult to decide whether early depictions of regions of the earth are maps or geometrical diagrams.

Early maps, where they had any measurements at all, had distances indicated directly on the maps. This is particularly noticeable on old nautical charts,[2] which frequently had the areas of seas crisscrossed with lines representing courses and distances to be sailed or bearings to be followed for particular periods of time.

The same applies to simple geometry today. A triangle may have the length of the sides and the angles directly represented on the figure:

Figure 11.6

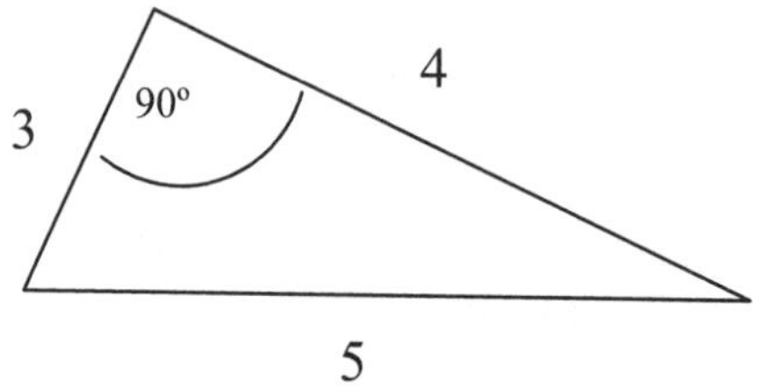

The sides don't have to be exactly three, four, and five units long, nor do they have to be accurately drawn to scale, and the angles don't have to be drawn very precisely either (especially for "rough work"). The geometry is not in the figure itself, but in the numbers.

BETWEEN SHAPES AND NUMBERS

In the early seventeenth century the French philosopher-mathematician Descartes had an idea that revolutionized both maps and mathematics. He put both geographical and geometrical diagrams into numerical frames. The numerical scales at the bottom and left side of a geometrical diagram or a map became known as *coordinates*, and the whole mathematical image was referred to as a *graph*. Descartes transformed mathematical thought with the insight that information about the dimensions and angles of geometrical figures need not be placed on the figure itself if the figure was appropriately located on a graph. Geometrical space could be reduced to numbers, just as the location of physical features of the earth could be reduced to numbers indicating latitude and longitude.

The coordinates that run across the bottom and up the left side of the border of the map represent position on the surface of the earth. (Sometimes the coordinates are repeated at the top and right side of the map, but this is merely for convenience; no additional information is conveyed.)

Encircling the World with Numbers

Here is a miniature map of a mythical island, with the coordinates of latitude and longitude indicated at the bottom and left side, respectively:

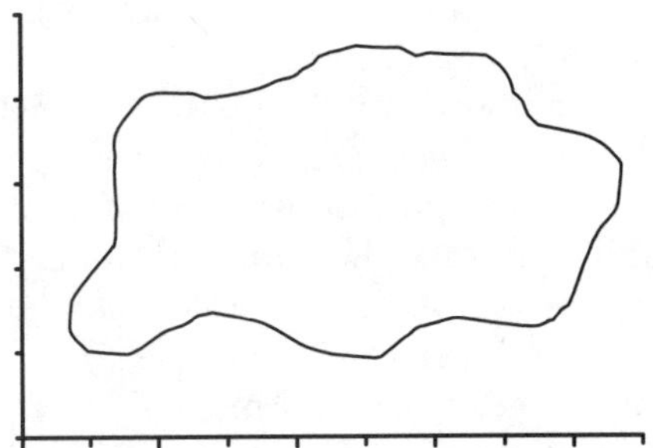

Figure 11.7

The coordinates permit any point on the map to be precisely located, and—once the scale of the map has been determined—they permit the distance between any two points of the map to be calculated. The idea of putting coordinates around the border of a map, usually seen as obvious today, took a long time to realize because of the problem of representing the entire globe, or large portions of it, on a flat surface. This is a geometrical problem for which a simple all-purpose solution has never been found, though fortunately the problem can be ignored for relatively small areas of the globe like cities, moderately sized countries, and mythical islands.

In geometry, everything that could be calculated from

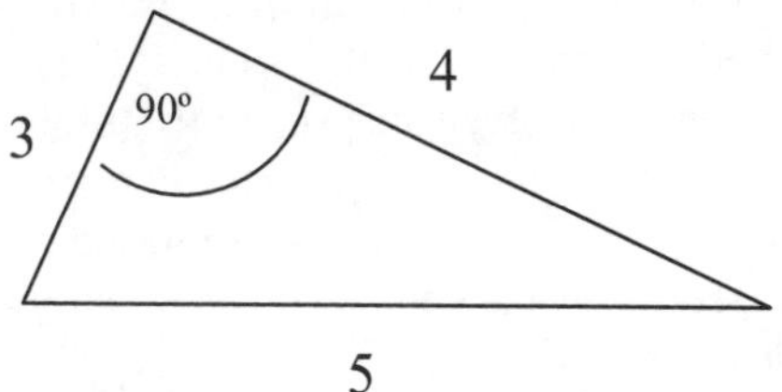

Figure 11.8

also could be calculated from

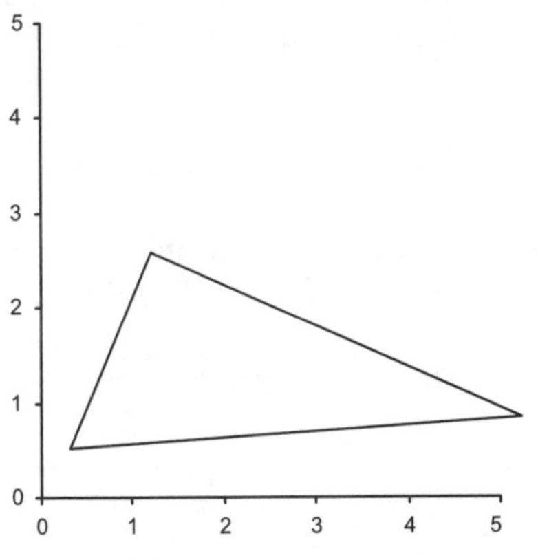

Figure 11.9

where the coordinates represent location in numerical space. One pair of coordinates could indicate a point in space—for example, (1,2) indicates one unit along on the x scale and two units up on the y scale. Two pairs could not only indicate the position of a line—(1,2), (2,3) meaning from (or sometimes through) (1,2) to (2,3)—but could also be the basis for calculating the "slope" of the line—the angle it made to the horizontal coordinate at the bottom. And three pairs of coordinates—(1,2), (2,3), (5,1)—could indicate an entire and unique triangle, with all its dimensions and angles open for calculation.[3]

Descartes's insight that geometrical forms could be expressed in numerical and algebraical expressions unified geometry and mathematics. It showed that the geometrical diagram—the representation of the world on paper—was essentially superfluous. All the truths of geometrical forms, once justified by eye, were now demonstrated to be a consequence of the consistency of numbers. Even in the world of shapes, numbers rule. (The same fact is demonstrated every time a calculator is used to solve a geometrical problem. A builder wanting to compute the pitch of a roof or the area of a wall need not put a diagram into the calculator; only the relevant numbers are required.)

But as we shall see, Descartes's demonstration that all geometry could be reduced to numbers did not make paper unnecessary for mathematicians. Quite the reverse; the demonstration also showed that relationships among numbers could be represented graphically. Graphs became maps of numerical landscapes, with inherent patterns that our essentially nonnumerical brains little understood and often didn't even suspect from numbers alone.

The substructures of mathematics were opened up to human eyes and understanding the way a geological survey map, or a chart of the temperature gradients of ocean waters, can reveal details and structures of hitherto unsuspected and inaccessible aspects of our physical world.

The mathematical power of graphs was more than a conceptual achievement. It could be argued that the consolidation on paper of geometrical and numerical aspects of computation made possible much of the scientific and technological developments of the following centuries.

FUNCTIONS

Throughout this book I have talked of relationships among numbers—the endless patterns in the tapestry of numbers—as the basis of all mathematics. The time has come to consider how different kinds of patterns can be brought together for our scrutiny, understanding, and service, in the compact form of *functions.*

The time also has come to introduce a small piece of formal mathematical notation that may be beyond the experience of some readers, the type of mathematical exotica that is often the source of anxiety and alarm. Yet the basic notation of functions is beautifully concise, wonderfully expressive, and immensely powerful. It is nothing more complicated than:

$$y = f(x)$$

where y is a number, and f is a signpost or indicator that the brackets contain a particular numerical pattern involving another number, x. (Letters of the alphabet are used, but this is not language; it is mathematical talk.)

The pattern that f(x) represents is formally called *the function of x*, or, even more concisely, the "eff of x." The statement y = f(x) says the value of y is always determined by the pattern of f(x). Let's say that the pattern f(x) is simply x + 2. Then when x = 1, y will be 3 (1 + 2). When x = 2, y will be 4 (2 + 2). And when x = 259, y will be 261 (259 + 2).

Functions reflect with exquisite economy the rich tapestry of numerical patterns that exist behind the glass wall. That is as much as the general reader need understand. Some examples will be found in the Notes.[4]

There are technical debates among mathematicians about whether functions should be regarded as rules, lists, statements of relationships, or simply another kind of number. Functions behave like numbers—they can be added, subtracted, multiplied, and divided—but they do other things as well. There is no point in arguing in *words* about the finer points of functions; functions are mathematical concepts, not linguistic ones.[5]

FUNCTIONS AND GRAPHS

Descartes not only revolutionized geometry with his conceptualization of graphs; he also explored mathematical functions, even giving them their name. So it should not be surprising that he was also a pioneer in plotting functions on graphs—putting numerical patterns on paper.

Here is a graph of the f(x) = x + 2 function I have just discussed:

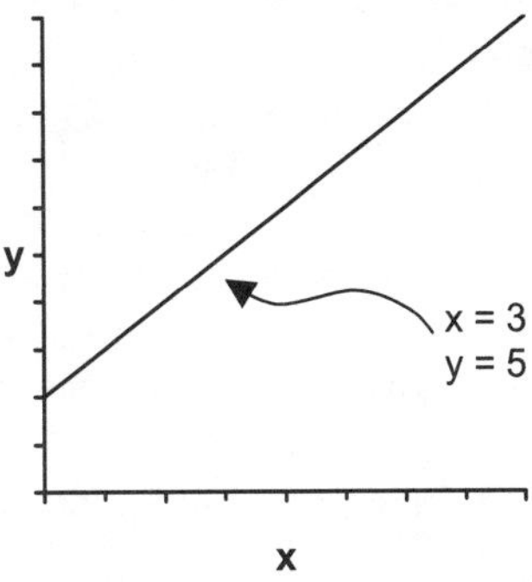

Figure 11.10

The vertical axis on the left is the *y* axis. It represents possible values of y. The horizontal axis along the bottom represents possible values of x. The graph is not complete, of course; it represents only a portion of the infinite number of values of f(x). Incidentally, the lines on graphs are usually called *curves*, even when they are straight. They represent potential locations in numerical space. Just as a train can appear anywhere on a railroad track, but nowhere else, so the values of a function can occur only along the curve of its graph. Two other examples are given in the Notes.[6]

As a final example of how relationships among numbers help to expand understanding of the world, I turn to the high school topic of trigonometry and those familiar but often confusing trigonometric ratios—*sines*. Victims of trigonophobia can safely skip this section of the chapter.

Trigonometry

Beginners usually learn that sines (and other trigonometrical ratios that will not be considered here) are relationships between the length of sides and size of angles in right-angled triangles. But rather than being concerned with particular dimensions, trigonometry focuses on *ratios*. Ratios remain constant. Triangles with sides of length (2, 3, and 5); (4, 6, and 10); (8, 12, and 20); and (5000, 7500, and 12,500) differ in size but their angles and the relative sizes are always the same. For geometrical purposes they are the same triangle.

Given the sine or certain other trigonometric ratios, you can look up in a table of trigonometric functions (or on a calculator that has been programmed with these functions) the value of an unknown angle. From a trigonometric ratio and the length of one side, you can calculate or look up the length of other sides. And from an angle, you can calculate or look up the sine and other trigonometric ratios.

From these enduring trigonometric functions all manner of matters can be calculated (or looked up), including the size of distant objects (whether trees on the horizon or galaxies in outer space), their distance from you and from each other, and the speed and direction of any movement they might have. For thousands of years trigonometric ratios have been the basis of all astronomy, surveying, map making, engineering, and navigation of the earth, seas, skies, and space.

Note what has happened. Numbers have been extended into space, and have permitted the discovery of all manner of things about objects in space. Only numbers have enabled this to be done. Some representation of the geometry involved may have been made on paper, but only to facilitate visualization of the relationships being examined. The calculation, and the discovery, is in the numbers.

The modern navigational aid known as the *global positioning system* (GPS) enables any person, on foot or in any kind of vehicle or vessel, to pinpoint a precise position on the earth, speed and direction of travel over it, and distance to any destination. The small receiver that is used calculates the bearings of satellites that constantly circle the globe, making instant use of trigonometry.

Did I say pinpoint a precise position on the earth? I mean position in space. The fact that the GPS receiver happens to be on the earth is coincidental. The orbiting satellites spin an invisible sheath of numerical space around the world, together with an invisible sheath of numerical time. Because of lumps and bumps in the surface of the earth and of the passage of the earth through time, small local corrections are always liable to be made. But the corrections adapt the earth to the numbers, not the numbers to the earth. Everyone today lives and moves in a world enveloped in numbers.

CHAPTER 12

Memorizing, Calculating, and Looking Up

Is mathematics something we know or something we do? The answer is both—mathematics is part facts and part acts. And there is no clear dividing line between the two. Instead there is a trade-off. When you make an excursion into the world of mathematics, the more you know, the less you have to do, and the more you can do, the less you need to know. Deciding which is preferable in particular circumstances has been a constant conundrum for mathematicians, educators, and the designers of scientific instruments.

Knowing something is relatively straightforward, though not always easy. You have to put something into memory (learning) and get it out again when you need it (recalling). For *doing* something you have two main choices. You can work out what you want to know (which entails knowing how to set about working it out). This is what usually is meant by *calculating*, and often can be laborious. Or you may be able to *look up* what you want to know, which used to mean consulting a set of tables or manipulating an abacus or a slide rule, but these days is more likely to involve a calculator or a computer. And there's another category that belongs under the heading of "looking up," even if the language is a bit contradictory, and that is the ancient and honorable procedure of asking someone to tell you what you want to know.

Cutting across all aspects of mathematical knowledge, calculation or looking up, is the inescapable matter of *understanding*, the only way to avoid running into the glass wall.

Shortcuts

One way to look at mathematics is to regard it as a complex system of shortcuts. In principle, everything mathematics lets us know and do could be done without any mathematics at all beyond counting—provided we don't run out of time, memory, patience, and brain power. Like the apocryphal shepherd, we could solve all our addition, subtraction, multiplication, and division problems by shifting around sheep, or more convenient counters of some other kind. But in place of the hard slog, we can rely on memory, calculating, or looking up what we want to know.

Let's consider a simple hypothetical problem that we can carry through this chapter. We would like to know what 14 × 14 equals. There's a nonmathematical way of solving this problem. We could set up 14 heaps of 14 pebbles, and count all the pebbles to see what the total is.

There's no mathematics in that procedure at all, either as fact or act, beyond counting. Even the result—196—need not be mathematical, since numbers by themselves don't have mathematical properties. Counting is the original brute-force way of solving arithmetical problems, frequently used spontaneously by children. Counting doesn't require any understanding of mathematical relationships beyond the number sequence. Memory, calculation, and looking up are all shortcut alternatives, and the amount of mathematical understanding they involve may vary from minimal to immense.

MEMORY

Memory, like understanding, is unavoidable in mathematics and everything else. Although mathematics might seem to be a constant process of "working things out," the foundation of any kind of mathematical enterprise is memory, and a great deal of learning mathematics involves committing mathematical facts and procedures to memory. Memory eases all of our way through mathematics, and we can't get started without it.

The most significant first step in becoming mathematical is to memorize, in their conventional order, the numbers from one to ten. These numbers are the building blocks of all of mathematics, and they are not something that you can work out for yourself, or look up when you need them. They have to be *known.*

Over and Under the Table

The next step in an individual's mathematical development is usually "tables"—for addition and multiplication. I'm not referring to printed tables with column after column of numbers arranged in a systematic way as a substitute for memorization, but packages of knowledge that must be committed to memory, sometimes in substantial portions but often a little bit at a time.

Tables, in this sense, are simply organized ways of remembering mathematical facts. Often they are in the form of a chant, which helps memorization. Thus:

One and one are two, one and two are three, one and three are four

and so on. Followed by:

Addition table

+	1	2	3	4	5	6	7	8	9	10
1	2	3	4	5	6	7	8	9	10	11
2	3	4	5	6	7	8	9	10	11	12
3	4	5	6	7	8	9	10	11	12	13
4	5	6	7	8	9	10	11	12	13	14
5	6	7	8	9	10	11	12	13	14	15
6	7	8	9	10	11	12	13	14	15	16
7	8	9	10	11	12	13	14	15	16	17
8	9	10	11	12	13	14	15	16	17	18
9	10	11	12	13	14	15	16	17	18	19
10	11	12	13	14	15	16	17	18	19	20

Two and one are three, two and two are four, two and three are five

and so on. And:

Three and one are four, three and two are five, three and three are six . . .

The addition table usually goes on as far as ten—*ten and ten are twenty*—making a total of 100 basic "math facts," illustrated above. Once memorized, these facts become immediately available for mathematical use. Provided, that is, that the nature of the facts and the manner of their use is understood—which requires further memorization.

Multiplication tables usually are recited and learned in the same way:

One two is two, two twos are four, three twos are six

and so on. Followed by:

One three is three, two threes are six, three threes are nine

and so on. And:

One four is four, two fours are eight, three fours are twelve . . .

The tables, once more, usually go as far as ten—*ten tens are a hundred.* The multiplication table, illustrated on the facing page, contains another

Multiplication table

x	1	2	3	4	5	6	7	8	9	10
1	1	2	3	4	5	6	7	8	9	10
2	2	4	6	8	10	12	14	16	18	20
3	3	6	9	12	15	18	21	24	27	30
4	4	8	12	16	20	24	28	32	36	40
5	5	10	15	20	25	30	35	40	45	50
6	6	12	18	24	30	36	42	48	54	60
7	7	14	21	28	35	42	49	56	63	70
8	8	16	24	32	40	48	56	64	72	80
9	9	18	27	36	45	54	63	72	81	90
10	10	20	30	40	50	60	70	80	90	100

100 facts, a total, with the addition table, of 200 facts that must be memorized before arithmetical calculation can comfortably begin.

The tables may not seem very impressive in themselves, child's play in fact, but they contain a substantial amount of useful information and a high degree of relational structure. A few simple rhymes conceal a detailed blueprint for the foundations of mathematics, as the preceding familiar illustrations reveal. (The tables as they are laid out in these illustrations are not things that need to be memorized. They indicate what *has been* learned if the addition and multiplication chants are familiar, displaying the mathematical information packed into the simple chants.)

Many fundamental mathematical and geometrical relationships are woven into the patterns of these tables, when the numbers are read horizontally, vertically, diagonally, or in leaps and bounds.[1] These blocks of numbers are probably a better illustration of the basic richness of mathematics than any unidimensional row of numbers.

At their simplest, these tables of elementary "math facts" replace calculations involving numbers less than ten—problems like 4 + 5 or 6 – 7—that otherwise would have to be worked out on fingers or with other kinds of counters. The fingers method might be called solving problems "under the table."

But the memorized tables are *essential* for calculations involving numbers larger than ten, or "over the table." If you don't know the addition and multiplication tables as far as 10, you're not going to be able to do calculations involving numbers greater than 10, like 19 + 37, or 14 × 78. The same applies to subtraction and division. And if you can't do these elementary calculations, you won't be able to do anything else in mathematics.

The heights of mathematics are scaled by standing on tables.

Procedures and Formulae

It's not just tables that have to be remembered. There are all kinds of procedures that also must be understood and retained in memory, beginning with multiple-digit addition and subtraction, and (possibly) long multiplication and division. And there are all kinds of formulae, arithmetical, geometrical, and algebraical, from the familiar to the abstruse, that are considered part of the knowledge of anyone expecting or expected to be familiar with mathematics at particular levels of competence.

Every procedure and every formula is a shortcut for working out a mathematical relationship. If you don't know the procedure and formula appropriate to a particular occasion, then you're going to have to do a lot more computational work, if you can, with the possibility that you'll get the wrong result.

The Mechanics of Memory

Memory is organized on the basis of understanding. Everything we remember is connected directly to something else that we know, and indirectly to everything else. Our memory of our telephone number is connected to our memory of telephones, how they are used and what they are used for. Our memory of the fact that Helsinki is the capital of Finland is connected to what we know about capitals and what we know about Finland. How well we remember anything depends on how richly connected it is to other things that we know.

This is why rote learning is both difficult and inefficient. It is much easier to remember things that are meaningful to us than things that are not. A person who understands prime numbers (divisible only by themselves and one) finds it much easier to remember the series 1, 2, 3, 5, 7, 11, 13, 17, and 19 than a person who does not. A person who understands a lot about mathematics generally finds it easier to remember more about mathematics; and a person who is confused by mathematics usually finds it impossible to remember anything about mathematics.

Not only is it easier to put mathematical facts into memory if they make sense to us, but it is also easier to get them out. Meaningfulness, or the richness of connections, determines how quickly and efficiently anything goes into memory, and meaningfulness, or the richness of connections, determines how quickly and efficiently we can get anything out again. For matters deeply related to significant aspects of our lives, both the learning and the recall are likely to take place without any conscious effort at all.

Where Should Memorizing End?

How much should be memorized? There's no limit to the capacity of memory, but learning takes time, and recalling can be difficult as well as pointless if we have stored away large amounts of stodgy knowledge that we haven't really made sense of. There probably is a limit to how much mathematical detail we *need* to remember—but that limit will differ with every individual.

A minimal kit for a basic mathematical memory would have to include the number "facts" for addition and multiplication up to ten, plus elementary procedures for simple calculations. What about our exemplary problem of 14 x 14? Many people remember facts about numbers greater than ten, not just for addition and subtraction but for many other mathematical purposes, simply as a result of interest and experience. But it is usually not possible or necessary to specify what these additional components of memory should be.

People who frequently multiply numbers between 10 and 20, especially if such calculations are an important and interesting part of their lives, will remember many double-digit multiplications, including 14 x 14, as easily as they remember their date of birth or their telephone number. People whose business or passion is numbers and their relationships, can remember them in vast quantities. A story often is recounted[2] of the self-taught Indian mathematician Ramanujan (admittedly a genius) as he lay dying at the age of 32. A visitor had commented that the license number of the taxi he came in, 1729, was "dull." On the contrary, said Ramanujan, 1729 was the smallest number that could be constructed in two ways by adding two cubes—$1^3 + 12^3$ and $10^3 + 9^3$. Ramanujan was as familiar with numbers and their habitats as ornithologists are with birds.

The question is not how big someone's memory is, or "how good" it is. What determines how well, relatively speaking, our memory functions in particular circumstances depends on the experience, interest, understanding, and *confidence* we can bring to what we are doing.

Memory for things mathematical makes a great difference to how easily anyone can behave in the world of mathematics, but efforts to memorize can be completely counterproductive when we have little understanding of what we are doing. That is one reason why mathematics suddenly can become frustrating and opaque, no matter how highly motivated we are. If we strive to memorize something we don't understand, if we're on the wrong side of the glass wall, we'll have great difficulty trying to remember it. But we'll have no difficulty remembering our failure and frustration—the underlying condition of any phobia.

CALCULATING

If you can't find what you want to know by referring to your memory, then you either have to work it out or look it up. Calculation, or working out, is the traditional, conventional, and educationally approved method of solving mathematical problems, even when these problems, especially when they are of the everyday variety, could be solved faster and more accurately by using electronic calculating devices.

Calculators often are regarded as something of a cheat in educational contexts (almost as bad as asking someone else for "the answer"). It sometimes is felt that students will be seriously handicapped if they don't work things out for themselves, even matters of considerable complexity and abstraction. "Do it yourself" is considered more admirable and beneficial than having someone else (or something else) do it for you.

But the issue is not as clear-cut as that. Doing things for yourself can be helpful—but only if it is accompanied by some interest, understanding, and success. Electronic labor-saving devices may have some disadvantages, but usually only when interest and understanding are lacking. Before venturing to consider the relative advantages and disadvantages of both working out and calculators, we should first look at them separately. For the sake of brevity, I will refer to "calculators" rather than the more long-winded "calculators and other electronic devices" or "computers and calculators."

The "Hands-on" Approach

What are the advantages of "do it yourself," whether with student worksheets and written problems, or with on-the-job calculations of dimensions, amounts of ingredients, or bank statements and shopping bills?

It is widely believed that doing something for yourself, with or without the assistance of other people, is likely to result in *learning* the mathematical procedure employed and the mathematical relationships involved. This may be true—as long as the learner understands what is going on and isn't distracted by complicated calculation. But what may be true for hands-on activities doesn't mean that the same end can't be achieved with calculators. Calculators don't necessarily take the place of thought; you usually need to understand what you are doing to punch in the appropriate numbers and procedures.

A second advantage of hands-on calculation is supposed to be *error recognition.* You may be more likely to realize that you have made a mistake or obtained an inaccurate result when it is part of something that you are working out for yourself than if you blithely read it off the display panel of a computing device. But if you know what you are doing, a result on a calculator may be just as obviously unrealistic as a result on paper. If you calculate that you need 50 gallons of fuel for a six-mile drive in the family car, you are just as likely to recognize that a mistake has been made whether the result appears in the window of a calculator or on paper.

A third possible advantage, not often talked about with respect to mathematics (or to much else that people often engage in learning), is *satisfaction.* Half an hour spent working something out can be far more interesting than a comparable amount of time spent putting numbers accurately into mindless devices and reading out meaningless results. But again, the reverse arguments also could be made, that calculators can reduce the tedium of computational chores.

There is no evidence that we remember more when we work something out for ourselves than when we look it up. Even "math facts" can be learned incidentally, during any kind of calculation. If it is important to us to know that $14 \times 14 = 196$ and we calculate or look up the result a couple of times in circumstances where we are not confused, then it probably will go into memory without effort. This is the way familiar telephone numbers or street addresses usually are learned, without deliberate memorization.

Anything we encounter while calculating (provided we understand and think about what we are doing) is more easily stored in memory, and more easily recalled when needed again, than things that we try to stuff away by drill and rote.

Unfortunately, children may be taught calculation by rote, with little understanding, and they may appear to be making great progress in mathematics while they are doing so. Many adults can do the same, with simple addition and subtraction and even basic multiplication and division. Then they run into the glass wall.

LOOKING UP

For centuries, the only alternative to making complex calculations for yourself was to look up what you wanted to know in tables—printed tables this time. The printing of tables was one of the earliest and most extensive uses of printing, from mathematical data of all kinds (squares, roots, logarithms, trigonometric ratios, and compound interest) to the daily state of the tides, stars, and planets.

The consultation of printed mathematical tables is still widely taught, or at least learners are exposed to it, but like the use of the slide rule, it is probably a dying art. Tables today are as likely to appear on computers and calculators as on paper.

Interestingly, tables that may appear to be "built into" (or "programmed into") calculators and computers may not in fact be there. Instead, the calculator works out specific values when required. The designers of electronic devices essentially have to make the same choice that we all make in mathematical matters—whether it is more economical to store facts (with the burden on "memory") or to work out what is required at the time (at the cost of speed). Electronic tide tables and tables of square roots, for example, are both worked out from recipes, cooked to order while we wait.

The "Punch-in" Approach

I noted earlier that students can learn from working things out for themselves if they are not distracted by complicated calculations. One advantage of calculators is that they readily perform complicated calculations—which often may be far more true to life. Textbooks tend to employ "easy" numbers—"a driver travels 3 miles at an average speed of 60 miles an hour . . . ," when a more realistic problem might be "a driver travels 3.7 miles at an average speed of 52.68 miles an hour." Scarcely any effort is involved in punching the extra digits into a keyboard, but the result may have an authenticity that immediately appeals to the learner, and prepares the learner for real-life applications and situations. The fact that easy numbers often are expected in textbooks also may encourage learners to make wild guesses or inappropriate assumptions about what correct results should look like.

Looking up can require as much prior mathematical understanding as working the same thing out on paper, plus knowledge of the way in which the calculating device has to be used. Even for 14 × 14, you need to know how to switch on the device in the appropriate calculation mode, understand the order in which to press the relevant keys, and know how to ask for and read the result that is given. Some technical or scientific calculators are particularly complicated to use. You can occasionally get results, even correct ones, without understanding the mathematics involved or the mathematical implications of the results obtained. But you can be in the same situation when making pencil and paper calculations.

There is an obvious risk with electronic devices that gross errors may occur because the person involved is not monitoring the calculation being made, and sometimes *can't* monitor the calculation. At a supermarket checkout counter, for example, the clerk may be passing bar codes in front of a sensor, placing produce on scales, bagging, and chatting to customers, while the register automatically tabulates items purchased, subtotals, totals and taxes, and prints out a detailed receipt.

Both clerk and customer may be unaware of potential errors when electronic calculators are employed at the supermarket. Yet electronic devices are used in all kinds of medical, judicial, financial, educational, and other bureaucratic contexts, to acquire, store, process, and act upon data that may never have passed before human eyes.

Complex computations like long division and taking square roots are no longer taught in many schools, because they are more easily and accurately performed by calculators. It is not clear what kind of loss this might be to learners. Many students in the past have run into the glass wall with long division, and many others learned how to perform the movements without understanding what they were doing. Computers and calculators routinely solve problems in compound interest that few people could work out in the past, and that they understood just as little when they consulted printed tables as they do today when the result appears on a monitor.

So is it a good idea to use calculators and other electronic computing devices in classrooms? I'm not trying to make an argument that calculators are always better or always necessary. But a puritanical rejection of their aid because they might make life too easy for students is not a realistic position from which to assess the role of electronic devices in classrooms or the role of classrooms in an electronic world.

CHAPTER 13

Getting Beyond the Glass Wall

Taking flight with a seaplane is a complicated business. The plane needs a substantial pair of floats to be stable on the surface of the water, but they become an encumbrance when the pilot wants to take off. The floats could create so much drag as the plane taxied across the water that it would not be possible for it to lift into flight, no matter how hard the engines labored. The solution is for a "step" to be built into the underside of the floats so that as the plane accelerates across the surface, the floats rise until they are almost out of the water, and drag is considerably reduced. Once a seaplane "gets on the step," as the pilots say, it is able to free itself from the water and climb into the air.

Learners have a similar problem as they try to soar into mathematics. Before they take off, they float securely on a surface of everyday language and familiar concepts. But to penetrate the world of mathematics they must escape the drag of the physical world, "get on the step," and break free into a totally different environment.

Unfortunately, it often happens that beginners seem ready to take flight—their engines are roaring as they labor across the surface—but they never take off into mathematical space. The students, and their teachers, may think the problem relates to progress through the water, but the real obstacle may be the inability to leave the water behind.

On Being Practical About Mathematics

I have never believed in telling teachers what they should do (though there's no shortage of individuals willing to do so). The practical reason for my reluctance to recommend particular activities, procedures, methods, and materials is my conclusion that mathematics shouldn't be taught as a sequence of prepackaged explanations, drills, exercises, and tests. There are no panaceas, or universal recipes.

Many teachers have little choice about the materials they use and the curriculum they follow. Yet their most critical practical concern must always be to understand the mathematical situation that the student is in. The issue is not so much what the teacher (or the textbook) is trying to teach as what the learner is learning. If the student is mistakenly learning that mathematics is confusing, or threatening, or forever beyond his or her competence, then such learning is obviously not to be desired. It is equally undesirable for mathematics to be learned as a set of ritualistic procedures and unconnected facts. The purpose of learning must be for the student to think like a mathematician, and that demands opportunities to explore and grow from a mathematical point of view.

Understanding Mathematics

When I use the phrase "understanding mathematics," I don't mean relating mathematical knowledge and procedures to the "real world." A few practical calculations can be made without any understanding of the underlying mathematics, just as a car can be driven without any understanding of the underlying mechanics. The learner can perform some mathematical moves, and even produce "right answers," especially after plentiful drills and exercises, without being able to generalize to other situations or to comprehend why mistakes are made.

The alternative, "understanding mathematics," means an appreciation of the relevant network of mathematical relationships, the numerical patterns that determine and justify applications. Contrasted with a child who can produce on demand the relevant "math fact" that $7 + 6 = 13$, another child who understands that $7 + 6$ is the same mathematical relationship as $10 + 3$, which is a self-explanatory way of thinking of 13, has learned to think mathematically.

Learners able to engage in simple counting and computation activities are usually regarded as demonstrating mathematical invention, creativity, exploration, and discovery. Unfortunately, this can be a delusion, for teachers and for students. Ostensible success in early counting and addition exercises (taxiing across the surface of familiar language and concepts) doesn't mean that children have learned anything mathematical (they have not taken off). Ostensible success doesn't even mean that children have learned what teachers assume they have learned—they may be doing something completely different. And finally, ostensible success in these early exercises doesn't mean that the children are developing a useful basis for subsequent progress in mathematics. Quite the reverse; we shall see that what children have unwittingly learned may become so deeply ingrained that they are fatally handicapped in subsequent efforts to make sense of relationships among numbers.

Learning Mathematics

Anyone can learn to understand and enjoy mathematics—provided they get beyond the glass wall and nothing goes wrong. That is my underlying premise. I should clarify first what I mean by "learning mathematics."

First, I don't mean learning all of mathematics. No one knows all of mathematics, and few people need to know what many professional mathematicians know, at least not in any detail.

And learning mathematics can't mean learning everything on a particular curriculum, almost certainly devised as a compromise of wishful thinking by a group of people far from the teachers and learners who will be directly affected. Specifying something on a curriculum doesn't mean it can easily be taught, learned, or understood. And attaining some specified standard on a curriculum is no guarantee that a mathematician will be produced. A curriculum is a blueprint for learning to be achieved, not a map for the best route into mathematics. Curriculum targets, objectives, or standards can be diversions rather than milestones.

The emphasis on use over understanding is explicit in "practical" curricula supposed to reflect the "needs" of the majority of students in their everyday lives rather than serve a "tiny minority" who might want to obtain advanced qualifications.[1] The patronizing dichotomy between an essentially nonmathematical mass and a small but elite minority is false and dangerous. The idea that the majority would be best served by a bundle of skills rather than by a deeper mathematical understanding would have the ultimate effect of closing off the world of mathematical understanding to most people, even those who might want to enter the many professions that employ technological or statistical procedures.

Being a mathematician is a state of mind rather than a repertoire of skills and knowledge. Becoming a mathematician should be an initiation, an affirmation, an induction into a club[2] that is open to all learners, no matter how limited their experience. Mathematicians can be distinguished by their constant readiness to learn more about mathematics; they are open to mathematical experiences, are unafraid of mathematical environments, and have a continual feeling and fascination for relationships among numbers.

The essence of mathematical learning has to be *continuity*, opening up rather than shutting down. Learning itself is continuous; it takes place over time. Insufficient time frequently interferes with learning things that would be learned easily if there were less haste.[3] It is better for the learner to be established on a secure beachhead than to be expected to reach arbitrary objectives according to arbitrary timetables.

How much mathematics should people be expected to learn? A few people will become virtuosos relatively quickly. A few will struggle to make small gains. Most people will be somewhere between the two extremes. The important thing is not how much mathematics can be learned in a given amount of time, but the learner's readiness and opportunities to explore mathematics in an interesting and stress-free way.[4]

Why Everyone Can Learn Mathematics

Learning is a natural and irrepressible activity for the human brain, and we all have the same kind of brain. We won't all achieve the same level of expertise—we differ in general abilities, energy, determination, interests, and experience—nor will we all learn at the same rate. But anything one person can learn, everyone can learn, at least to some degree.

Mathematics isn't in your genes, nor is it wired into your brain cells; it hasn't been around long enough in human history. We can't get mathematics from another person in a transfusion. Mathematics is a combination of human discovery and human invention. If we can learn anything, we can learn mathematics. Whether we want to learn, or think we can learn, is another matter. Anyone can learn negative attitudes. Anyone can learn phobias.

In fact, we can't help learning. The problem with any formal instruction is not that students don't learn but what they learn. It is the nature of the human brain to look for the three *C*s—consistency, coherence, and consensus—in every situation. If students encounter mathematics in circumstances they find inconsistent, incoherent, and contentious, that is what they will learn about mathematics.

Evidence that students are learning, often in the most enterprising ways, is provided by the inventiveness that they display, even when they may be getting everything wrong. As I will shortly show, children who encounter the most difficulty sometimes invent the most ingenious strategies.

Invention can be regarded as the "step" that takes learners beyond the constraints of the physical world and natural language into the open skies of mathematics. Learners must lead with their imagination, and will always strive to do so. Children often give correct answers for the wrong reasons, and when they give incorrect answers their errors are usually systematic. In both cases they have tried to find an appropriate understanding. There are more examples of learner inventiveness, both "correct" and "incorrect," later in this chapter.

As I reiterate, anyone can learn to understand and enjoy mathematics provided nothing goes wrong. And nothing will go wrong provided four essential conditions are met. These conditions can be stated so succinctly that I put them into the following compact list:

Four Essential Conditions for Learning Mathematics
1. The mathematics must be interesting and comprehensible
2. There's no fear of mathematics
3. Inappropriate things aren't learned
4. There's sufficient time

1. Interest and Comprehension. The first essential condition for learning is easily expressed but not always easy to achieve in a classroom, or even in solitary study. The *situation* in which the learning is to take place must be interesting and comprehensible.

It is not just that boring or incomprehensible material is more difficult to learn. What is learned is that the material is boring and incomprehensible, no matter how much others tell us they find the same material fascinating and clear, or how *useful* it might be to learn it.

Interest attaches us to a situation; it engages our attention and focuses the imagination. Comprehension provides the links that enable us to attach something new to everything we know already. With boredom there is no engagement, and with incomprehension there is aversion.

Some teachers and curriculum designers seem to regard boredom and confusion as the learner's problem, as if learning could still take place if the learner tried harder. And certainly, boredom and lack of comprehension are enormous problems for teachers compelled to teach a subject, no matter what the students think about it.[5]

But unfortunately, making material interesting and comprehensible *is* the teacher's role. Students learn what they experience. And that begins with the most fundamental lesson of all, the learning of fear.

2. Learning Fear. Fear is the first of the inappropriate things that must *not* be learned if the glass wall is to be circumvented. No one is born afraid of mathematics—or regarding it as boring, incomprehensible, or difficult. Experience teaches us what we should fear, just as it teaches us what we can't do.

Sometimes we get such negative experience at first hand. We find ourselves in a situation where we feel under threat—perhaps, for example, because we believe that our performance on an examination will result in feelings of inadequacy, incompetence, or humiliation. It is not difficult to make anyone feel uncomfortable and inept, especially a child who has no control over prevailing circumstances. One of the easiest and most common ways of creating anxiety is the frequent use of tests, designed specifically to discover where teachers and students are "failing," so that they can be "held accountable" for their own lack of understanding.

But it is just as easy and far more common for people, especially children, to become afraid or apprehensive from the way they see other people behave.

Teachers and parents who find mathematics boring or incomprehensible easily convey those feelings to a child. Teachers and parents who themselves fear exposure to mathematics easily transfer the fear. Children don't necessarily learn what we hope we are teaching them, but they are most susceptible to learning what we unwittingly demonstrate.[6]

3. Learning Inappropriate Things. You can learn inappropriate things about yourself—or about mathematics. The most general inappropriate thing you can learn about yourself is that you can't do mathematics. The most general inappropriate things you can learn about mathematics are that it is boring, alien, bewildering, and a cause for anxiety—you have gone beyond the familiar territory of language, but you are not at home in the world of mathematics. Your nose is pushing against the glass wall.

There are also many specifically inappropriate things that can be learned about mathematics, starting with the widespread conviction that mathematics is based on counting, and extending to such misconceptions of detail as the belief that addition and multiplication always make two numbers bigger, or that fractions have to be treated differently from whole numbers. I give further details below.

Such misconceptions may become dangerous when teaching ties mathematics to operations with "familiar objects," in "authentic situations," with everyday language. Teaching of this kind may help young students make apparent progress across the surface, but never allow them to get on the step to take off into the realm of mathematics.[7]

4. Time. Learning can't be forced. Mathematics is not something that can be learned in a hurry, especially if the learner finds it difficult or confusing. It is absurd to expect everyone to learn mathematics at the same rate, yet the constraints of today's approaches to education often put students and teachers in a time-bind. Students who "fall behind" can rarely catch up, and their task is always harder for them. The weakest students get the most homework. They have more learning to do, less time, less success, and less encouragement than students who can move forward just a little bit faster. The gap between students who are good at mathematics and those who are not grows wider as they progress through the educational system.

And at examination time, the students who don't think they have enough time are the ones most likely to panic and least able to think constructively.

DRAWING FROM THE MATHEMATICAL MIND

Constructivism as a psychological theory asserts that knowledge—and therefore understanding—is not a property of the physical world, but something that has to be constructed by each individual. Explanation doesn't create knowledge or understanding. Everything we know and think must be constructed and tested in our own mind. This is not to say that we can create any kind of knowledge that we like—we usually (though not always) test our theories against our experience and against the theories of other people. We look for coherence, consistency, and consensus. But knowledge can't be put into anyone's mind. It must come from insight and reflection, even when we are simply thinking about something we have been told.[8]

The constructivist stance is that mathematical understanding is not something that can be explained to children, nor is it a property of objects or other aspects of the physical world. Instead, children must "reinvent" mathematics, in situations analogous to those in which relevant aspects of mathematics were invented or discovered in the first place. They must construct mathematics for themselves, using the same mental tools and attitudes they employ to construct understanding of the language they hear around them.

For example, Constance Kamii, a leader in constructivist mathematics instruction, argues that addition doesn't need to be taught. First graders can construct the relevant logical mathematical knowledge on their own when engaged in such activities as equalizing small stacks of counters. Kamii wants children to learn as a result of their own thinking, not from "facts," and when involved in situations in daily living, in voting, and in board and dice games, as well as in discussions of computational problems.

Kamii is the author of three books with the title of *Young Children Reinvent Arithmetic* (or *Young Children Continue to Reinvent Arithmetic).*[9] A former student and colleague of Jean Piaget, she shows how mastery of numbers and of numerical operations can develop spontaneously with the progression of children's "scientific thinking." And logical, scientific thinking, she argues, arises from children's *reflective abstraction* from their own actions. Kamii urges that children should be autonomous in their learning, to encourage them to think, and she also stresses the importance of social interaction. Conflicting ideas, like incorrect responses, may be necessary if higher levels of understanding are to be attained. She is highly critical of "tricks" and "algorithms" that are taught without concern for comprehension, such as telling children to calculate an average by first adding all the relevant numbers, or to multiply 80×8 by first multiplying 8×8 and then adding a zero, when they can't see any sense in the initial steps.[10]

None of this means that children should be left to their own resources to recapitulate 5000 years of mathematical history, including all of the false turns and blind alleys. But it does assert that children can and must invent mathematics for themselves if given opportunities for relevant experience and reflection.

MAKING MATHEMATICS DIFFICULT

Learning anything that makes sense to us is not difficult. A struggle to learn is always a struggle to make sense, and when we learn something, we learn it only in a way that makes sense to us (no matter how it might appear to someone else). What we learn, and can't help learning, is the particular ways we manage to solve or skirt around problems. If we find a strategy that works for us, that is what we learn. And what we learn can't be erased. Bad habits are as persistent as good ones.

Children's inventiveness doesn't necessarily lead to productive conclusions. Children can learn the wrong thing. Some examples follow.

Counting on Counting

The assumption underlying many "practical" approaches to instruction is that counting is at the heart of mathematics. Children must first learn to count (acquire a "number sense"), then gain an understanding of the base system and the place system, master "simple" operations (addition, subtraction, multiplication, and short division), and memorize a number of "math facts" (addition and multiplication tables) and some elementary geometry. They will then be in a position to apply mathematics in practical situations and to go into deeper aspects of mathematics, including fractions and decimals, algebra, further geometry, exponents, and logarithms. Unfortunately, counting is about as far as many learners get—and their reliance on counting prevents them from getting any further.

The idea of counting usually comes easily for children because the ideas involved (one, more, all) are rooted in everyday language and everyday experience. Simple problems in addition, and in due course in multiplication and subtraction, often are solved through spontaneous variants of counting.

Addition frequently begins as a simple continuation of counting—the process known as *counting-on*. Asked to add 3 and 2, children start from 3 and use their fingers to "count-on" two more numbers: "four, *five*."

Soon many children are able to dispense with the use of fingers, but count-on mentally—"four plus three is five-six-*seven*."[11] By counting-on, learners can add double-digit numbers without having to worry about carrying or place: "eight plus four is nine-ten-eleven-*twelve*"; "twelve plus four is thirteen-fourteen-fifteen-*sixteen*." In effect, such learners have no conception that numbers beyond nine are any different from the numbers preceding them—even if they have to be written with two digits. They do not understand the base system.

The problem may be aggravated by the fact that the numbers from ten to twenty don't *sound* as if they are any different from numbers below ten.

Twenty one, twenty two, and so on, sound like combinations of smaller numbers, as do two hundred and two, and two hundred and thirty four. But ten, eleven, twelve, thirteen . . . nineteen, twenty sound like indivisible wholes.

Counting-on is almost universal. Children often invent the procedure spontaneously for themselves, or are quick to adopt it from other children or from their teachers. Because of the immediate success with simple exercises that counting-on can bring, some teachers teach the procedure in the belief that it will help children make progress in mathematics. For a brief while, this may seem to be the case.

Children who count-on usually realize or learn quite rapidly that the efficient way to perform addition through counting-on is to do so from the larger number. Asked to add 3 and 9, they will count-on three from nine rather than nine from three. Once again, they appear to be gaining mastery, but in fact they are exploiting a clever shortcut for getting correct answers that gives them only short-term gains.

Such children also have little problem in generalizing the procedure to subtraction, accomplished by "counting-down": nine take away three is eight-seven-*six*, surreptitiously counting off three on their fingers, or in their imagination.

The mind-set engendered by counting-on that ten, eleven, and twelve are an uncomplicated continuation of seven, eight, and nine may not reveal any difficulties until children are presented with written problems involving double-digit numbers.

Children by then may have little idea of what is involved in "carrying" in double-digit addition or "borrowing" in double-digit subtraction. Either they regard the columns as separate single-digit problems, or they become confused over what to do with the extraneous digit:

37	37
+18	−18
45 (or 415)	29 (or 21, subtracting smaller from larger numbers)

They haven't understood that the digits in the "tens" position (such as the 3 in 37) are not numbers that can be counted-on from (or counted-down from), like the digits in the units position; numbers in the tens position are different kinds of numbers, despite the similarity of their appearance, whether they occur set out vertically in "sums" or simply appear in numbers of two or more digits in isolation (37 or 200). This is not a question of conventions or of procedures; it is a matter of relationships.[12]

Efforts to teach about base and position independently from counting may then have little success because children lack a framework on which to understand what the teacher is talking about (even if they learn to parrot what the teacher says). With their ingenuity they can discover or learn ways to give right answers without understanding why they are doing what they do.

This is not a trivial matter. It is not resolved by stressing the mechanics of carrying and borrowing. The problem is not what the children have failed to learn (the base and place systems) but what they have already and indelibly learned—that all mathematical problems can be solved by counting.

Failures to understand the base and place systems are only two of the problems that come to confront children who learn that addition is counting-on and that subtraction is counting-down.

When "More" Should Be "Less"

The belief that addition means "more" and that subtraction means "less" leads eventually to problems with negative numbers. Addition of a negative (4 + -1 = 3) makes a positive number smaller, and subtraction of a negative (4 – -1 = 5) makes a positive number bigger. This is incomprehensible to many people who have not gone beyond the glass wall into the world of mathematics. They may memorize the "rules" sufficiently to be able to recite them; they may even be able to carry out the procedures from time to time; but they will never understand. What can be done about this? More "explanation" won't help and rote memorization will be futile. The immediate solution must be to postpone the instruction, whatever the curriculum demands, until the learner is comfortable in the world of mathematics, with patterns among numbers.

There are similar problems with the idea that multiplication is repeated addition, and division repeated subtraction. Multiplication by a number smaller than 1 creates a smaller number (4 × 0.5 = 2); while division by a number smaller than 1 creates a larger number (4 ÷ 0.5 = 8). This again may be counterintuitive to children (and to many adults).

The conviction that multiplication results in a larger number leads to confusion with many "real-world" problems, for example, temperature conversions and currency exchange rates. Converting from degrees Fahrenheit to degrees Celsius involves multiplying by 5⁄9 (or roughly 0.6), something many nonmathematicians are reluctant to do. Many people have no trouble multiplying a price in U.S. dollars by (say) 1.5 to get the equivalent in Canadian funds, but they balk at *multiplying* a Canadian dollar amount by 0.67 to get the approximate U.S. dollar equivalent. They feel that 0.67 and other numbers less than 1 call for division.

Many children refuse to divide a smaller number by a larger one, so a typical strategy with two numbers is to multiply if the second number is larger than 1 but divide if it is smaller than 1. They have no trouble calculating the cost of 3.5 liters of juice at $1.25 a liter, a relatively simple matter of multiplication, but can't work out 3.5 liters at $0.75 a liter—they want to divide.

All of these problems arise because children become convinced that addition and multiplication mean "more" and that subtraction and division mean "less." These early conceptualizations are difficult to overcome. They may not be conscious, but they provide a false foundation on which to build more complex mathematics. And with this constant failure comes inevitable discouragement and a conviction that the individual does not have the right kind of mind (or brain) for mathematics.

Children also have frequent problems reading some multi-digit numerals. They can manage 47, where the "four" part is uttered before the "seven," but have difficulty with 17 or 217, where the numbers are not spoken in the order in which they are written (or counted). They also have problems with any number with a zero in it (2007 or 207), because zero is not a counting number.

For the same reason, many children have difficulty understanding that fractions are numbers; we don't normally count in less than wholes.

Children must learn that with the exception of numbers between 13 and 19, multi-digit numbers are read from left to right (like sentences in written language), although calculations proceed in a right-to-left direction (add, subtract, or multiply the units before the tens, and the tens before the hundreds)—except in the case of division, where everything is performed from left to right.

All of these things, which seem obvious to anyone who can do them (though they may not know the reason for the particular directionality), are confusing and even irrational to many learners.

The solution to all these pedagogical problems frequently is seen as instruction and practice specifically applied to the procedures that the student is having difficulty with. If the learner has difficulty carrying, or multiplying by numbers less than one, carrying and multiplication by numbers less than one should be *taught*, with lots of repetition and feedback, according to this common view. But the real problem may go much further back, to the fact that in acquiring the initial basic skills of single-number addition and subtraction, children learned things that could only interfere with subsequent learning.

The counting point of view makes whole numbers seem "easier" than other numbers. There is a preference for problems like 2.8×6 rather than the identical 6×2.8, and similar transpositions may be made in division (preferring $2.8 \div 6$ to $6 \div 2.8$), where the reversal makes a substantial difference.

Counting strategies enable learners to accomplish the tasks set for them by the teacher and instructional materials, but they may achieve this in ways that the teacher doesn't suspect or doesn't realize will become a serious handicap in subsequent efforts.[13]

Ironically, what makes children look competent in basic-skill exercises quickly proves to be a handicap in their subsequent progress. They find ways of making good speed across the water, but never get enough lift to take off.

The dilemma that confronts teachers in their efforts to understand what is going on in children's minds also confronts *researchers,* who may not be examining what they think and claim they are investigating. The predicament is not improved by the fact that both evaluation and research tend to focus attention on aspects of mathematics that are "obvious" and easy to count or measure.

Problems with Words

It is widely believed that mathematics can be made more meaningful, and mathematics instruction more effective, if mathematical procedures and problems are wrapped in the form of everyday language. There is a concern that children should feel comfortable with using simple numbers and simple numerical operations in "authentic" natural language situations.

But there are doubts whether many "word problems"—embedding (or hiding) mathematical applications in "stories"—do much to improve mathematical comprehension.[14] Such problems need to be carefully designed and used in ways that encourage children to develop relevant computational techniques. Otherwise, children easily but unwittingly subvert teachers' aims by showing the same originality and inventiveness they demonstrate in purely mathematical situations.

For example, they will solve word problems (often successfully) by the clever invented strategy of looking for key words. "More" is taken to mean add and "less" to mean subtract.[15] They will be guided by the size of numbers, the kinds of numbers, and number of numbers that appear in the problems to determine whether they should add, subtract, or multiply.[16]

Children may appear to gain mastery but in fact find practical shortcuts and signposts that eventually constitute obstacles to future progress. They usually prefer their own invented procedures to formal procedures that they don't understand.

Some children will do almost anything to avoid reading and analyzing the language in their attempts to solve word problems. There may be good reason for this. Mathematical structures are not easy to uncover in word problems, and the same mathematical problem may be embedded in different linguistic structures. Reading ability alone is not enough to solve word problems,[17] nor is proficiency at computation.

Errors usually are made consistently, not because the students aren't thinking, but because they quickly find the key word they are looking for. Students who make the most correct responses (and higher-ability students) often need more time, because they are reflecting more.[18]

Another prominent means of trying to make early mathematics practical is to engage children in *estimation* activities. It is true that practical adult mathematics often involves estimation—in budgeting, assessing quantities, keeping running totals while shopping, tipping, and checking change. But estimation is not a part of mathematics; it is a specialized application. Mathematics is concerned with precision, and trying to teach estimation as part of mathematics confuses many children and leads to frequent efforts to avoid it. A popular invented strategy for children in estimation problems is to do an exact calculation first and then round up or down.

Many preschool children are able to make sense of addition and subtraction problems even when they can't see the evidence—for example, when asked how many children there will be in a shop if two are already there and two more go in. But give the same children the same problem in formal mathematical notation (2 + 2 = ?) and they may be unable to make any sense of it.[19] Children also may have particular trouble with the equals (=) sign: They think it is an instruction to do something.[20]

Fostering a Mathematical Mind

Because mathematics must come from the mind of a learner, it follows that no set or sequence of instructional principles will guarantee learning. What matters is whether the learner is confused or discouraged by encounters with mathematics.

Failure with an instructional method doesn't mean that a child is incapable of mathematical understanding; it means that the child—at that time, and with those materials—is confused or perplexed. Such a failure doesn't require that the child should receive intensive instruction or practice on the part of the instructional program that is causing difficulties, but rather that the difficulty (for the learner) of this particular part of the program should be identified and avoided. Unfortunately this is often not the view of the teacher, who regards the occasional difficulty most children have in learning as a challenge, or the view of the curriculum. And many parents don't help. They survived mathematics instruction in school, so why shouldn't their children?

Just as failure doesn't mean inability, so success, in the form of correct answers, doesn't guarantee that a child is learning anything useful or productive. The transient good feeling of getting high marks or grades collapses when followed by the inability to cope with more complex encounters. "Math panic" is seen as a persistent cause of failure, often resulting from the learning of technique without understanding.[21]

Children may be overwhelmed by being confronted with too much at once—for example, large numbers and the place system. They can be crippled by fear of failure, by repeated immersion in what they don't understand, by lack of time, and by extraneous worries, for example, about spelling and neatness, testing and grading. Most early remedial and tutorial efforts emphasize numbers and counting. They frequently fail to recognize that mathematics can't be explained in everyday language or learned by rote, that what looks obvious to the teacher may be far from obvious to the student, and that the ability to do something doesn't necessarily mean understanding.

Many kinds of difficulty confront learners. Locating these difficulties in the learner's brain and giving them pseudo-medical names is not helpful. Usually what is needed is more time, more understanding, more sensitivity, less pressure, a fundamentally different approach to mathematics education, stressing comprehension rather than memorization—and sometimes a period of mental convalescence.

"Helpful hints" for teachers don't help either. It is insulting to teachers to suggest that their troubles would go away if only they changed their methods. They must instead sensitize themselves to recognizing whether all their students, the "successful" ones as well as the others, are operating in a world of remembered bits of language or the world of mathematics.

Everyone has a mind capable of mathematical thinking. Whether or not particular individuals develop their potential depends largely on their initial encounters with the world of mathematics, and with the glass wall.

Notes

INTRODUCTION

1. Mathematics today is much more than numbers, but numbers were the beginning of mathematics and are the way everyone gets involved in mathematics. There is no reason in this book to venture far beyond the numerical threshold to mathematics.

2. Even mathematicians can make this assumption. Keith Devlin opens his beautiful book *Mathematics: The Science of Patterns* (1997) with the offhand assertion, "To recognize the pattern that we call 'threeness' is to recognize what it is that a collection of three apples, three children, three footballs, and three rocks have in common. 'Can you see a pattern?' a parent might ask a small child, showing her various collections of [three] objects'" (p. 9). There is more on this in Chapter 3.

3. Walkerdine (1988). Elsewhere, she notes that "volume" may not be a concept of capacity to children, but a button on a television remote control (Walkerdine, 1982).

4. The word *mind* and the word *brain* occur frequently in my discussions. Pedants sometimes argue that there is a difference between mind and brain — that the brain is an organ and the mind a function of that organ, or that the brain exists in the physical world and the mind in a mental one. Some will assert that the mind is a fiction constructed by the brain (or that the brain is a fiction constructed by the mind). On the other hand, many languages don't have separate words for mind and brain, saving their speakers the trouble of having to think about such weighty matters. The distinction between mind and brain is linguistic, a matter of convention. Dictionary definitions disclose nothing about the physiology and psychology of human thought and behavior.

English is particularly rich in different and sometimes overlapping usages for the words *mind* and *brain*. We talk of changing our mind, not changing our brain. But we have brain waves, not mind waves. We bear something in mind but tell people to use their brain. We can have a tune on our mind or running around in our brain (as well as in our head). We have mind-sets but brainstorms. We have mindless acts but are brainwashed. It is commonplace these days to talk of the brain learning, thinking, and understanding, but this is more metaphorical than scientific (and may be done simply to sound scientific). It would be equally appropriate and often more apt to talk of a person, rather than a brain, learning, thinking and understanding. The colloquial ways in which the words *mind* and *brain* are used arise from linguistic chance.

CHAPTER 1: WHAT IS MATHEMATICS?

1. Mathematical statements aren't ambiguous, but they may refer to more than one mathematical state of affairs. The square root of four (either 2 or -2) is an uncertainty but not an ambiguity.

2. I don't want to suggest that the imprecision of natural language is a flaw. Permeable boundaries allow growth, novelty, and the eternal possibility of saying something new. In fact, specialists in some recondite areas of mathematics have introduced the notion of "fuzzy logic" to permit going beyond constraints that strict mathematical logic would impose on them (McNeill and Freiberger, 1993).

3. Because of the "s" on the end, the word *mathematics* might be thought to be plural—"mathematics are" rather than "mathematics is." But the *ics* suffix is singular, indicating an area of study or common interest (as with physics, athletics, or ethics), and is derived from Greek and Latin suffixes roughly meaning "pertaining to." The "s" wasn't present in earlier words like music, arithmetic, and logic, although *ic* has a similar derivation and semantic function to *ics.* The transition from *ic* to *ics* occurred when academic specialists began demarcating territories they wished to claim for themselves, mainly in the sixteenth century.

4. Arithmetic used to be what children did in grade school, one of the three Rs. Educational hyperbole has inflated reading, writing, and arithmetic into literacy, communication skills, and mathematics.

5. For a detailed research account of the sophisticated homemade mathematics of child candy sellers in the Papua New Guinea highlands, see Saxe (1991). For descriptions of informal adult use of mathematics in supermarkets, see Lave, Murtaugh, and de la Rocha (1984).

6. Field (1989) describes the "fictionalist" point of view that mathematics is a good story. Like many stories, it may be true of the world in certain circumstances. The same author (Field, 1980) asserts that it would be possible to have science with stories but without numbers, though he acknowledges that mathematics is good as an instrument in ways that stories are not.

7. For an interesting and idiosyncratic view of how mathematics might have evolved from the kind of thinking that makes language possible, see Devlin (2000).

8. Mathematical knowledge is part of the world of ideas and knowledge that philosopher Karl Popper (1972) characterized as "world three," in contrast to the

external physical world that we inhabit and the internal world of individual feelings and beliefs. Knowledge in world three exists not only in books but in artifacts in general. An automobile reveals many aspects of what we know about automobiles, about metals and electronics, and about mathematics. World three is created by people—not all at once, or all in the same place, but a little at a time, in the way that the world of music has been created—and it exists independently of people.

9. My own preferred conjecture is that mathematics generally had quite a different provenance, among stars rather than sheep. For ancient people, stars would have been the most prominent, familiar, yet inexplicable part of the landscape, a constant source of wonder and late-night entertainment. Always changing position, but always returning to where they were before, stars were beyond the reach of human beings yet intimately connected with human affairs—with the tides, the weather, and seasons of birth, death, and growth (not to mention being the home of the gods). The cosmic cavalcade would have been a fertile ground for exploring numbers and their properties, the patterns in spatial relationships, and the recurrence of events. But this is just a personal predilection for one story, or fable, over another.

10. There is more on children's reinvention of mathematics in Chapter 13.

CHAPTER 2: MAKING SENSE

1. For more extended discussions of this point of view, see *to think* (Smith, 1990) and *The Book of Learning and Forgetting* (Smith, 1998). I don't regard such arguments as "I don't have that kind of brain" valid. We all have the same kind of brain, though our talents, interests, and experience inevitably differ. We all have potential—though not *equal* potential—to be musical, mathematical, or anything else. Music, mathematics, and everything else that humans have created, are all within our competencies, to varying degrees. But they are not in our genes.

2. Bruner (1997) proposes that three "primitive" (or basic) modes of thought enable us to make sense of the world: *intersubjectivity* (reading other people's minds; understanding how they speak, act, and perceive the world); *actional* (constructing narratives to describe and explain actions, agents, and purposes); and *normative* (establishing standards, conventions, obligations, and other expectations). Making sense, or "meaning making," says Bruner, is a matter of interpretation, usually appropriate to particular situations and "highly tolerant with respect to verifiability, truth conditions or logical justification" (p. 283). He also proposes a fourth mode of meaning making, *propositional*, in which rules and symbols are used to achieve "decontextualized" meanings (or meanings that can be abstracted from particular situations and generalized).

3. Consistency also embraces *continuity*, the idea that experience will never be

disjointed, and that everything will be followed by something else in its appropriate place. Continuity is an important mathematical concept.

4. The word "categorize" requires some qualification. There's a tendency to think that categories are like shoe boxes or file folders, neatly lined up with no space between them and no doubt about where any particular thing should be placed. But it is often difficult to decide into which category an object or event belongs. Should dawn be placed in the category of day or of night, or in a category of its own—which still won't help you decide when night ends or day begins? This is more "fuzzy" thinking (see Note 2, Chapter 1). It might be better to think of categories as hooks on which things that bear a certain similarity are placed, leaving room for smaller hooks in the spaces between. Language (usually) might be thought of as providing hooks for categorizing schemes, while mathematics (usually) provides more clearly defined boxes. For more on the topic of human categorization, see Rosch and Lloyd (1978) and Huttenlocher, Jordan, and Levine (1994).

5. I analyze how human minds are extended by interaction with paper—how what is in the mind and what is on paper continually change and elaborate each other—in an examination of composition in *Writing and the Writer* (Smith, 1994). See also David Olson's *The World on Paper* (1994).

CHAPTER 3: THE MATHEMATICS IN LANGUAGE

1. There is evidence that people were recording number (in the form of notches on fragments of bone or stone) around 12,000 B.C.

2. Many historical references are available on the development of picture writing. Olson (1994) and Harris (1995) are particularly interesting. Several contributors to Senner (1989) propose that written language could have derived from mathematical writing (calendars, astronomical data, commercial and official records), and both from drawing.

3. Even before they utter their first words, infants are very sensitive to differences and changes in the relative rates of movement (Bower, 1971), a concept at the heart of calculus.

4. The writing, erasing, and rewriting of two alternative characters on an endless strip of paper is the basis of Alan Turing's revolutionary concept of a "universal machine." Many discussions of this profound idea are mathematically and philosophically complex, but there is a readable overview in Hodges (1985).

5. Don't bother with the following amplification unless you remain unconvinced that showing three pencils and then another two doesn't demonstrate that three plus two makes five. Suppose you are in a foreign country, knowing nothing about mathematics or the local language, and someone holds up a bunch of pencils and says to you, "Here are glerp pencils." What could glerp possibly mean? Could the speaker be referring to the color of the pencils, or their size, or their

ownership, or whether they are beautiful or ugly, cheap or expensive, good to eat or poisonous? How could you decide from your past experience that glerp means a certain *number* of objects (remember, you don't have a prior understanding of numbers)? And if you don't understand what glerp means, how would you understand a demonstration that glerp pencils and strag pencils make grunk pencils? It wouldn't help if the speaker was enunciating the words clearly and waving the pencils around emphatically, the way we are all tempted to do when conversing with someone who doesn't have the faintest idea what we are talking about.

You might object that since glerp, strag, and grunk are totally alien words, there's obviously no way the pencil demonstration would work. But supposing you were familiar with the words, the way that children are familiar with one, two, three, four, five. The children have been taught to *count*, and are very good at saying the words in the correct order. Surely then the demonstration would work. But suppose the foreigner uses familiar words in my pencil example. Suppose we are told, "March pencils plus February pencils make May pencils"? Could we then understand the "explanation," because we have learned the words January, February, March, April, and May by heart and can say them in the correct order? The familiarity of the words doesn't clarify the mathematical concepts; in fact, it makes the demonstration more confusing. Children don't learn the meaning of numbers by being shown "concrete" examples of those numbers, or rather examples of how those numbers can be used in the physical world. How do children learn the meaning of numbers? The precise details of this feat are a little complex (or counterintuitive) and it will take time to spell them out at an appropriate place later in the book. Briefly, children don't learn the meaning of numbers by launching themselves from the world of pencils to the world of mathematics; rather they have to develop their understanding of numbers in the world of mathematics, which they can then use to make sense of demonstrations with physical objects. I don't deny that children can be *trained* to give the correct response to "problems" in the 2 + 3 = 5 class, just as a dog might be trained to bark the appropriate number of times in similar situations. But being able to *perform* a correct response in relatively simple situations doesn't mean that any mathematical understanding has been gained. I probably could learn to glerp, strag, and grunk enough to fool a few people in the foreign country, but that would be no indication that I had learned anything productive about the language or the country. It wouldn't get me behind the glass wall.

6. Even very young children are able to draw logical conclusions of this kind in situations that are meaningful to them (Nelson, 1985). But this doesn't mean that children will necessarily give correct answers to "logical" questions, especially if the questions are in unfamiliar language or presented in the form of deliberate puzzles or test items. Conversion of the Ann, Ben, and Carol situation to abstract form—"if A > B, and B > C, then A > C"—creates particular difficulties for children, and for adults as well, but not because they are unable to reason "logically."

When underlying patterns of thought have familiar contexts stripped away, transposed into specialized systems with their own language and notational conventions, they become in effect distinct "worlds." And people may encounter a glass wall that makes it impossible for them to enter such a world, even though in familiar circumstances they can think logically.

7. Lakoff (1987).

8. This is the basis of the controversy over the year in which the third millennium began, 2000 or 2001.

9. Reasons why simple counting could itself be a handicap are elaborated in Chapter 13.

10. There is a similar problem in reading instruction, with learners unable to understand such expressions as *letter, sound, word,* and *sentence* until they can read (Smith, 1999).

11. *Diagonal* is a particularly challenging word, though used with abandon in many discussions of geometry, because there is evidence that children have difficulty even in *seeing* diagonals, and in copying them (Olson, 1970). The word is rarely used in everyday language, perhaps because we don't normally encounter diagonals except in artwork and the design of flags. The dictionary offers "oblique" and "slanted" as definitions for diagonal, which hardly fill the mathematical bill.

CHAPTER 4: THE MEANINGS OF NUMBERS

1. It is common to attribute a sense of number to children—and even to animals—because they are able to discriminate between different quantities. But the fact that birds, chimpanzees, and infants can distinguish between collections of 2, 3, and 4 objects, and even indicate that one collection is larger than another, doesn't mean they have any notion of numerosity. It simply means a sensitivity to size, to amount, to magnitude. One problem is that it is almost impossible for numerate adults to think about quantity without thinking about number, and it is absolutely impossible to talk about quantities with precision without using numbers. (We can talk of a small group or a large group, but that doesn't distinguish groups of 2, 3, or 4.) The word *quantity* is often taken to be synonymous with number. Research indicating that animals and children can distinguish different quantities often attributes to them an innate sense of number when the most that might be said is that they have a nonnumerical sense of quantity. Stanislas Dehaene frequently refers to quantities as "numbers" in a broadly researched book entitled *The Number Sense* (1997)—although he puts the same term in quotation marks in the text and insists that he doesn't think the brain contains an "arithmetical unit" predestined for numbers and mathematics.

Huttenlocher, Jordan, and Levine (1994) showed that children by 5 or 6 years of age can answer simple addition or subtraction questions or solve simple story problems such as adding or taking away two marbles. But children as young as 2 can solve similar problems *nonverbally*, without conventional calculation skills, for example, by indicating the correct number of items when they see two items added to or taken away from a group that has been hidden from them after they have seen how many there are. Children can do this approximately at about 2 years of age, but exactly—nonverbal calculation—about six months later, when "symbolic play" (where one thing stands for another) begins to be exhibited.

2. Roland Barthes (1980) argues that numbers don't have meaning in stories, only in mathematical contexts. He gives the example of fictional secret service agent James Bond picking up one of four telephone receivers on his desk. Barthes says the word *four* functions in the story only as a referent to a "highly developed bureaucratic technology." It would have made no difference if there had been five or nine telephones; the number has no mathematical relevance.

3. Woodworth and Schlosberg (1954, p. 94) and Mandler and Shebo (1982).

4. There may be a few exceptions. Expressions like 24 hours, 48 hours, and even 72 hours have established themselves in the language as synonyms for a day, two days, and three days. But for 48 hours to be numerically meaningful, it would have to contrast with periods of 47 hours or 49 hours, not 24 or 72, and I can't imagine many circumstances in which such a contrast might arise. Are such conversions of days to hours more scientific, more authoritative, or just blarney? I mention this because I have just heard a politician stating that an "emergency" unit would be ready to move at 96 hours' notice.

5. In the North American counting system, billions come cheap at just a thousand million each (1 followed by 9 zeroes). In the United Kingdom, France, and Germany, a billion is a thousand times larger at a million millions (1 followed by 12 zeroes). The European billion is called a trillion in North America (a thousand North American billions, or 1 followed by 12 zeroes), while the European trillion is a million European billions (1 followed by 18 zeroes). Such monumental discrepancies in terminology among major countries, when so much else is "standardized," can be explained only if these enormous numbers are meaningless, even to the people using them. When the numbers are written for mathematical purposes, which is the only time their exact meaning really matters, there is no computational confusion, only total detachment from everyday reality. In this book, the North American conventions for billions and trillions are respected—as if it made the slightest difference.

CHAPTER 5: NUMBERS (I): THE NAMES

1. Even newborn infants are responsive to the difference between two or three objects, or sounds. They show surprise if they encounter more or fewer than they

have been led to expect (Dehaene, 1997, Ch. 2). But they seem to be estimating rather than counting, responding to numerosity, not number.

2. There have long been arguments about the precise reason why children have difficulty with Piaget's "conservation of number" problem, focusing on the unfamiliarity of the language and experimental setting. For fuller accounts, see Hughes (1986, Ch. 2), Beilin (1976), and Donaldson (1978).

3. The possible historical priority of the ordinal system may be indicated by the fact that English (though not all languages) has unique words for "first" and "second" that are not derived from the corresponding cardinal terms "one" and "two." "Third" lies in an intermediate category, and from then on the ordinal always consists of the cardinal with the simple addition of "th"—fourth, fifth, . . . nineteenth, twentieth, . . . hundredth, thousandth . . . . A similar independence can be found with English adverbs referring to numbers of occasions or events. There are unique words for once, twice, and perhaps thrice, rather than one time, two times, and three times, but then the cardinal system takes over again—four times, eight times, ten thousand times. For a detailed analysis of the distinctive linguistic forms of small numbers, see Hurford (1987).

4. Many abacuses, including those in use today, have five counting beads on each wire plus an additional couple to indicate whether the five are being used a first or second time. Thus the abacus functions on a base-10 system, though only seven beads are used on each wire. The wire-and-bead abacus is a relatively modern (fourteenth-century AD) Chinese invention. Before that the Chinese used bamboo tallies and chips for computations. Elsewhere a variety of forms of ruled tablets (slates, boards, table tops) and "counters" (coins, buttons, pebbles) were employed as forms of this universal device. The checkered tabletops used for computational purposes in Britain were the origin of the term Exchequer for the government finance department—and for the word cheque (or check) itself.

5. Called a *mil* because each $\frac{1}{6400}$th part of the circumference of the circle is approximately a thousandth of a radian (which is equivalent to the radius of the circle).

6. Computer technologists have introduced a few hybrid terms for nonmathematical purposes, like "bytes" (for groups of eight binary digits), followed by kilobytes (a thousand bytes), megabytes (a million bytes), and nanobytes (a billion bytes). These inventions combine the nomenclature of two systems, the binary and the decimal, for the purpose of conversation, but are useless for precise calculation in either system.

CHAPTER 6: NUMBERS (II): THE WRITTEN FORM

1. I refer to "left-to-right" as the order in which both numbers and letters are written (but not necessarily read) because that is the convention of the English

language, which I happen to be using. It would be cumbersome always to write "left-to-right, right-to-left, up-and-down, or down-and-up, whatever the convention might happen to be," but that is what should always be assumed. I similarly assume that the abacus to which I refer is constructed or placed horizontally, so that the wires and lines and beads form rows, not columns.

2. For an erudite and engaging discussion of the widespread consequences outside mathematics of the introduction of the number 0, see Rotman (1987). Harris (1995) says that zero has nothing to do with language. It was the solution to an alignment problem in written mathematics before it acquired mathematical value as a number.

3. There is a widespread intuitive belief among students and teachers that $0 \div 0 = 0$. Tsamir, Sheffer, and Tirosh (2000) found that the mathematical prohibition on division by zero collided with the intuition that every mathematical operation should result in a number, leading to frustration and incomprehension. Only mathematical reasoning can explain why division by 0 must always be undefined—that as the divisor gets smaller, the result gets bigger until it approaches infinity, which is also not a number. Efforts by students and their teachers to explain the reasoning by concrete examples or everyday logic (nothing divided by nothing must be nothing) are counterproductive.

4. Kline (1980, pp. 114–116, 118).

5. Numbers above and below zero on thermometer scales sometimes are employed to explain positive and negative numbers. But the dividing line between positive and negative numbers for temperatures is arbitrary, depending on where the zero is placed. Temperatures represented by negative numbers between -10 and 0 on the centigrade scale, for example, are represented by positive numbers between 0 to 32 on the Fahrenheit scale. Minus 4 degrees is not the opposite of plus 4 degrees, whatever the scale we are working with. Temperatures themselves are never negative (though they may be intolerable), only the numbers.

6. The adjectival and verbal forms have different histories. The idea of negative numbers, with all its difficulties, has been around for at least 2000 years, but according to my dictionary, the first use of – as the sign for subtraction occurred in 1673.

CHAPTER 7: LABELING, ORDERING, AND QUANTIFYING

1. I'm talking of "whole" numbers here. The point will be clarified later.

2. Innumerable research studies have been done of children's counting and their understanding of what they are doing. Two scholars whose earliest reports are still influential in the field are Gelman and Gallistel (1978). See also Gelman (1979).

3. Holmes and Morrison (1979).

4. Carey (1978).

5. Cromer (1971, cited in Holmes and Morrison, 1979, p. 212). Holmes and Morrison observe that while children have to strive to make sense of time, they have no corresponding difficulty with space. They quickly learn about the solidity of objects and how to negotiate their own bodies between them. The visual sense of perspective is built in.

CHAPTER 8: CALCULATING AND MEASURING

1. For consistency in the present chapter, I refer to a complete mathematical statement (such as 9 + 6) as the *expression* of a relationship. In everyday language such an expression might be put into words like "nine plus six" or "nine and six" or "nine added to six." And what in everyday language might be referred to as the "sum" or "result" or even "answer"—all misleading terms to some extent—I refer to neutrally as the *value.* The mathematical value of nine plus six is fifteen. The word "value" also implies "meaning"—the mathematical meaning of nine plus six is fifteen. When mathematics is written, the value is indicated by the "=" sign, usually referred to in speech as "equals," "is," or "makes." Calculation is the determination of the value of a mathematical expression.

2. The less common words *aggregation* or *conflation* would be more precise than *combination,* because the latter might suggest "separate but together," while the mathematical effect of addition (and multiplication) is to make a single larger whole out of smaller wholes.

3. See preceding note.

4. As I observed in Note 9, Chapter 1, the sky was much more interesting and important in ancient times than today. The stars (far more brilliant in the sky, and far more familiar than they usually are today) served as clocks, calendars, almanacs, compasses, direction signs, and repositories of stories and rules for living. The arcane knowledge of the movements of stars and planets, and of the mathematics that was used to describe and predict these movements, was commonly in the hands of priests, who therefore could exercise great influence in earthly as well as spiritual affairs.

5. The earth-based calendar year of 365-and-a-bit days, derived from the annual journey of the earth around the sun, couldn't be used anywhere else in the universe. You have to be on earth to experience what we call a day, from one sunrise to the next. The joint effect of the earth's daily rotation around its own axis daily while the earth as a whole circles the sun once a year means that any one particular spot on earth faces the same configuration of stars in the night sky 366-and-a-bit times a year. This additional day, which is important in navigational calculations, is referred to as the sidereal day. Sidereal time is time as seen from the stars.

6. There have been fruitless proposals to move the division of time closer to a metric basis, for example, with 10 "months" in the year, 10 "days" in the week, and ten 100-minute "hours" in the day, each minute with 100 seconds. Metric seconds, minutes, and hours would have a different duration from our current ones, but in principle there is no reason why such a conversion should not be made. While astronomical considerations can be disregarded in the decimal divisions of the day, they would still make mathematical havoc of the year. Each of the 10 metric months would have to consist of 36 days (3.6 metric weeks)—and there would still be about 5¼ days left over.

7. Technically I should be talking about mass, not weight. Mass is a specified amount of matter, and weight is the way that mass is measured. The distinction is a fine one that has not made its way into everyday parlance.

8. The determination of a degree as equivalent to $\frac{1}{360}$ of the distance around the circumference is arbitrary, based probably on an approximation of the number of days in the year, and related to nondecimal methods of counting with a base of 60 rather than 10. There are alternatives. Geometricians and other specialists tend to make their angular calculations in terms of radians (which equal the proportion of the distance around the circumference of a circle corresponding to its radius).

CHAPTER 9: NOTATION—SIGNPOSTS IN THE WORLD OF MATHEMATICS

1. Semioticians—specialists who study notational systems—draw a technical distinction between signs and symbols, reserving the former for cases where there is a physical resemblance or connection of some kind, and the latter for arbitrary or conventional associations. But no individual or group can legislate how people in general use language. Nor is there much wrong with the way people in general use language, provided they are understood by the people they are addressing. Increased—and essentially artificial—precision has its cost. It requires either draconian laws about language use, which few people would tolerate, or more words. The philosopher Karl Popper (who always wrote succinctly and lucidly) said that extra precision in language could be achieved only at the cost of clarity (1976, p. 24).

2. To be even more precise, *people* represent relationships through notation. Kamii (1985, 2000) has pointed out that pictures, groups of objects, and mathematical signs or symbols don't represent anything. The word "three" and the number 3 don't represent three of anything, or even the idea of threeness; the number 3 is used or taken by people (in the case she is discussing, children) to represent whatever idea or function of three they have in their mind. So when I am talking about notation representing anything, this is a shortcut for saying that people rep-

resent ideas through notation.

3. The Arabic word from which the term originates is *al-jabra*, which refers to the setting of a broken bone. The metaphorical leap from a surgical procedure to the use of letters in place of numbers is too convoluted even to consider.

4. There are still occasions when the sign is omitted in multiplication, for example, with algebraic symbols (6X means 6 × X), and in front of braces—6(2 + 3) means 6 × (2 + 3).

5. The + sign does have a literal heritage, though it would be difficult to guess it today. In the Middle Ages, + was derived from the letter *t* in the written word *et*, meaning "and" (which might well be a better name for the sign than "add").

CHAPTER 10: NUMBERS BETWEEN NUMBERS

1. There is one inexorable restriction on fractions. They may be regarded as ratios or proportions between any two whole numbers, no matter whether they are positive or negative—provided that neither of the numbers is zero. It is an illicit operation in mathematics to divide any number by zero because there is no way of computing the result. So you can't have a fraction like $\frac{1}{0}$ or $\frac{5}{0}$. Dividing by 0 doesn't make sense, so mathematically you aren't even permitted to think about it. Nor can you have a fraction like $\frac{0}{1}$ or $\frac{0}{5}$, because nothing divided by any number is similarly unthinkable. The same restriction, of course, applies to ratios; nothing can be proportional to 0.

2. The ratio of the circumference of a circle to its diameter is the celebrated number called pi (represented by the Greek letter π). Pi exists somewhere between $\frac{22}{7}$ and $\frac{22}{8}$. If you know the diameter of a wheel is exactly one meter, then you know that the circumference is—*approximately*—$\frac{22}{7}$ (or 3.142) meters. You can calculate the circumference to as great a degree of accuracy as you like, to 10 or 100 or an infinite number of decimal places, but you can never achieve absolute precision (the way you can assert that $\frac{21}{7}$ is exactly 3) because the calculation of pi itself never comes to an end. You can't escape the predicament by arbitrarily giving an exact measurement to the circumference of the wheel, for example, by saying that it is precisely 3 meters. If you do that, you'll find you can't calculate a precise number for the diameter. Either way, you get pi in your face.

There is a similar dilemma with the diagonal of squares. Imagine a perfectly square paving stone, each side of which is exactly one meter. The unshakable theorem of Pythagoras says that the length of the diagonal, squared (multiplied by itself), must be equal to the combined squares of the other two sides. Since each side is one meter long, the length of the diagonal is the square root of one squared plus one squared, or the square root of two ($\sqrt{2}$). And there is no fraction that expresses exactly the value of $\sqrt{2}$, which in decimal form lies somewhere between 1.414 and 1.415. You can achieve as much precision as you like by extending the number of decimal places—but you can never hope to reach an end. It doesn't help if you double the length of each side to two meters, so that the length of the diagonal is the square root of 2 squared plus 2 squared ($\sqrt{8}$). Eight doesn't have an exact square root, nor does any other number that is the sum of 2 equal squares (for the simple reason that the sum of two equal squares must always contain two as a factor, and the dreaded square root of two doesn't exist!). And once again the problem can't be resolved through the back door. You can't give a whole number to the diagonal and then calculate the length of the sides. You will again find yourself entangled in the tentacles of $\sqrt{2}$ and unable to come to an exact mathematical conclusion.

Numbers like pi and $\sqrt{2}$ can be used in calculations (which inevitably end up being approximate), they can be put into numerical order among other numbers, but they can never be precisely identified. With good reason, perhaps, such numbers are called *irrational.*

CHAPTER 11: NUMBERS IN SPACE

1. For a brief history of maps, see Chapter 10 of Olson (1994), whose title, *The World on Paper*, suggested the heading for this section. Olson's phrase "the view from nowhere" was the title of an earlier book by Thomas Nagel (1986).

2. "Map" usually refers to a representation of land areas of the world, or the entire world. "Chart" is the word for representations of bodies of water and the surrounding coastlines, or for expanses of space. Sailors, aviators, and astronauts use charts; people traveling over the solid surface of the earth use maps.

3. To keep the numbers simple, I have employed coordinates in my discussion of the triangle in Figure 11.9 that do not correspond to the triangle illustrated in Figure 11.8. More precise values would do the trick.

4. We could compile a list that says at much greater length exactly the same thing as $y = f(x)$ when $f(x) = x + 2$ (the dots indicate that the series continues):

when x = 1 2 3 4 . . . . 259 x

y = 3 4 5 6 . . . . 261 . . . . x + 2

Both the list and the function represent the mathematical pattern established by adding 2 to every number. Obviously the functional notation is more concise and uncluttered; it says all that is necessary and nothing that is irrelevant.

Functions can get as complicated as you like (and some of the functions that mathematicians deal with can get very complicated indeed). Here is a relatively simple function that describes the pattern by which miles are approximately related to kilometers:

$$y = f(x) = 1.6x$$

(where y = distance in kilometers and x = distance in miles)

In list form:

when x (distance in miles)	=	1	2	3 . . .	259 . . .	x
y (distance in kilometers)	=	1.6	3.2	4.8 . . .	414.4 . . .	1.6x

And here's a slightly more complicated function that relates degrees centigrade to degrees Fahrenheit:

$$y = f(x) = \tfrac{9}{5}x + 32$$

Thus if x = 0 (zero degrees, or freezing point, centigrade), then $f(x) = (\tfrac{9}{5} \times 0) + 32$, which equals (since anything multiplied by zero is zero) just 32, which is of course freezing point on the Fahrenheit scale. And if x = 100 (100 degrees, or boiling point, centigrade), then $f(x) = (\tfrac{9}{5} \times 100) + 32$, which equals 180 + 32, or 212, which is boiling point on the Fahrenheit scale. And the comfortable temperature of x = 20 (20 degrees on the centigrade scale) is $f(x) = (\tfrac{9}{5} \times 20) + 32 = 36 + 32 = 68$ degrees on the Fahrenheit scale. (See Figure 11.n2.)

There are some restrictions on the kind of numerical patterns that can be functions, but that kind of detail can be left to mathematicians. Other letters of the alphabet may be used to represent variables, and other letters, apart from f, may be used to indicate functions when more than one is being considered (though f is invariably used as the first or only function).

5. David Berlinski (1997), who writes very eloquently about calculus, says nonetheless that "mathematics isn't *palpable*" (p. 67); it can't be put into words. His particular example: You can't say what a function is and you can't say what a function does; it is what it does and it does what it is.

6. Here is the graph of the function relating miles to kilometers, f(x) = 1.6x:

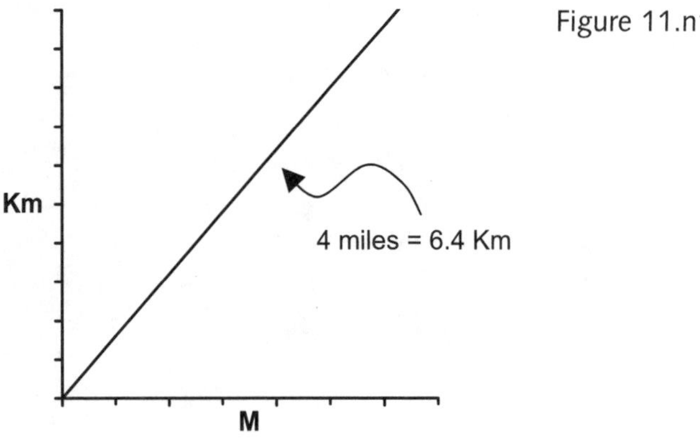

Figure 11.n1

And here is the graph of the function relating degrees centigrade to degrees Fahrenheit, $f(x) = \frac{9}{5}x + 32$:

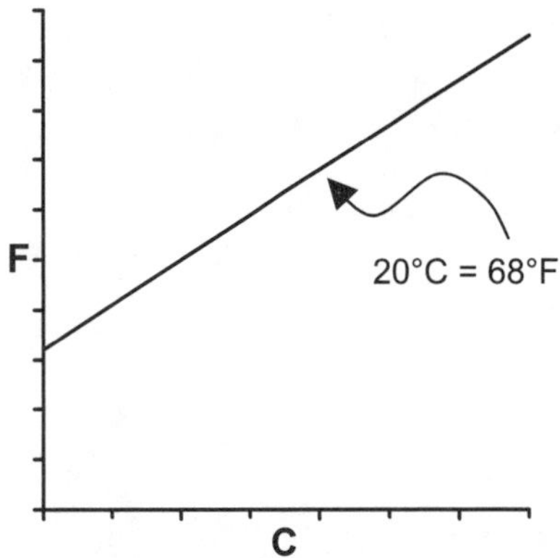

Figure 11.n2

CHAPTER 12: MEMORIZING, CALCULATING, AND LOOKING UP

1. In the addition table, for example, see how the diagonals from top left to bottom right increase in twos from top to bottom (4, 6, 8 . . . 5, 7, 9 . . .), while the diagonals from top right to bottom left remain constant (4, 4, 4 . . . 5, 5, 5 . . .), suggesting a rigidity in the structure of addition relationships that is almost tangible. The main left–right diagonal (2, 4, 6 . . .) is the two-times multiplication table, while the three-times table can be detected on a flatter diagonal (3, 6, 9 . . .). Every number from 1 to 20 seems solidly in place, folded neatly on the line of 10s on the main ascending left–right diagonal, with no exceptions. The multiplication table, on the other hand, is full of holes. There is no sign in this table of a prime number greater than 2 (such as 3, 5, 7, 11, 13, 17 . . .), as though the multiplication table is a sieve that excludes prime numbers. And indeed, one of the ways in which mathematicians (and computers) calculate prime numbers is through an ancient procedure known as Eratosthenes' sieve. Interesting numbers are easily found in the fabric of the multiplication table, including the squares (on the main diagonal from top left to bottom right—1, 4, 9, 16 . . .). Follow any diagonal *up* from left to right and see the numbers soar and then descend (8, 14, 18, 20, 20, 18, 14, 8), while the diagonals *down* from left to right increase in stately progression (4, 10, 18, 28, 40, 54 . . .).

2. For example, Dehaene (1997, p. 148).

CHAPTER 13: GETTING BEYOND THE GLASS WALL

1. My example is taken from the British national curriculum, discussed by Greer and Mulhern (1989).

2. The argument is developed in *Joining the Literacy Club* (Smith, 1988) and *The Book of Learning and Forgetting* (Smith, 1998).

3. See "Just a Matter of Time" (Smith, 2001).

4. I could make similar arguments for learning music, sailing, a foreign language, or astronomy. What matters always is not the actual amount of ground covered but the pathways that are opened up.

5. Of course, many children and older students declare that a situation is boring as a way of expressing unwillingness to follow someone else's agenda. Unfortunately, the fact remains that teaching something that is found boring, even out of perversity, demonstrates only that the subject is boring (and that perversity pays off). The problem is not that students refuse to display interest just because we would like them to, but that the educational system often requires (or at least expects) that teachers teach and students learn in situations that are mutually boring and frustrating.

6. Not surprisingly, students with "math anxiety" tend to feel tension, panic, and impending crisis when entering a mathematics class, undermining both their interest and performance. Karan Smith (2000) summarizes recent research in a report on a community college course in beginning algebra that combined traditional instruction with "nontraditional" help to students with negative attitudes toward themselves and mathematics. When their unsettled states were taken into account, many students reported feeling less anxious about their abilities to cope with their anxiety and mathematics, and more confident about learning.

7. Why do children who are otherwise intelligent exhibit poor performance in school mathematics? Ginsburg and Allardice (1984) showed the main cause to be lack of understanding of mathematics and of mathematics instruction. The children had adopted or learned incorrect procedures or principles—what the authors called "gaps, informal skills and bugs" (p. 209). The research showed that such children could think mathematics was arbitrary and make wild guesses because of panic or anxiety. They could have problems with rigid instruction and tests, confusing textbooks, and the discouragement of independent thinking and of idiosyncratic styles. The authors concluded: "These children are not cognitively defective, they are poorly educated" (p. 218).

8. An accessible introduction to constructivism from an educational perspective is Fosnot (1995). See also Saxe (1991).

9. Kamii (1985, 1989, 1994, 2000). The examples and assertions in this section were all drawn from Constance Kamii's work.

10. Kamii refers to conventional rules for mathematical procedures, like "carrying" and "borrowing," as *algorithms.* Her research showing harmful effects of teaching algorithms in the first four grades, and compatible findings from many other parts of the world, are reported in Kamii and Dominick (1998). For other volumes discussing ways in which teachers try to generate mathematical thinking through problems and discussions, see Cobb and Bauersfeld (1995) and

Carpenter, Fennema, Franke, Levi, and Empson (1999).

11. Baroody (1987). See also Baroody (1995).

12. Place value is very difficult for first graders. In fact, barely half the children Kamii studied in grade 4 and only 78 percent in grade 8 understood that the 1 in 16 chips meant 10 chips (Kamii, 2000, p. 81).

13. The difficulties that can arise when counting is adopted as the basis of mathematics have long been recognized. A common alternative is to teach some form of *regrouping*, by which numbers involved in basic mathematical procedures are reorganized into new patterns, often centering on multiples of 10. These new patterns reduce the need for children to count-on and bring to their attention the interlocking structures of numbers. For example, instead of being taught (or encouraged) to calculate 7 + 6 by counting-on directly to 13, students would first increase the 7 to 10 (by taking 3 from the 6) and then add the remaining 3 to achieve the total of 13. Similarly, 14 – 5 would be computed by taking 4 from the 5 to reduce 14 to 10, and then deducting the remaining 1 to reach the solution of 9. With familiarity and understanding, regrouping is not as complicated as it might seem. Many children regroup spontaneously. Adults may do the same when adding long columns of figures, without being aware of exactly what they are doing. Regrouping can avoid some errors of carrying and borrowing, and it also has the advantage of reorganizing numbers into groups in which mathematical patterns and structures become obvious and productive. (See Kamii, 1985, 1989, 1994, 2000.)

14. There is a popular idea that mathematics learning will take place only if children talk about "problems," but this depends on whether there are any insights to talk about. Interesting arguments on both sides concerning the value of embedding mathematical problems in stories are in Bickmore-Brand (1990). Wood (1988) asserts that "making mathematics 'relevent' to children by invoking everyday imagery may serve not to simplify their problems but make them more difficult" (p. 199). See also Backhouse, Haggarty, Pirie, and Stratton (1992).

15. De Corte and Verschaffel (1989, p. 94).

16. Mangan (1989, p. 115).

17. Mangan (1989, p. 113).

18. Mulhern (1989, p. 36).

19. Hughes (1986, Ch. 3).

20. Hughes (1986, Ch. 7).

21. Buxton (1991).

References

Backhouse, John, Linda Haggarty, Susan Pirie, and Jude Stratton (1992). *Improving the Learning of Mathematics.* Portsmouth, NH: Heinemann.

Baroody, Arthur J. (1987). *Children's Mathematical Thinking: A Developmental Framework for Preschool, Primary, and Special Education Teachers.* New York: Teachers College Press.

Baroody, Arthur J. (1995). The role of the number-after rule in the invention of computational shortcuts. *Cognition and Instruction, 13*(2), 189–219.

Barthes, Roland (1980). Introduction to the structural analysis of narratives. In A. K. Pugh, V. J. Lee, and J. Swann (Eds.), *Language and Language Use.* London: Heinemann Educational Books. Also in Shirley Brice Heath (Ed. and Trans.). (1977). *Image—Music—Text.* London: Fontana/Collins.

Beilin, Harry (1976). Constructing cognitive operations linguistically. In Hayne W. Reese (Ed.), *Advances in Child Development and Behavior* (Vol. 11). New York: Academic Press.

Berlinski, David (1997). *A Tour of the Calculus.* New York: Vintage Books.

Bickmore-Brand, Jennie (1990). *Language in Mathematics.* Australian Reading Association.

Bower, Thomas G. R. (1971). The object in the world of the infant. *Scientific American, 225,* 30–47.

Bruner, Jerome S. (1997). Will cognitive revolutions ever stop? In David Martel Johnson and Christina E. Erneling (Eds.), *The Future of the Cognitive Revolution.* New York: Oxford University Press.

Buxton, L. (1991). *Math Panic.* Portsmouth, NH: Heinemann.

Carey, Susan (1978). The child as word learner. In Morris Halle, J. Breslin, and George A. Miller (Eds.), *Linguistic Theory and Psychological Reality.* Cambridge, MA: MIT Press.

Carpenter, Thomas P., Elizabeth Fennema, Megan Loef Franke, Linda Levi, and Susan B. Empson (Eds.). (1999). *Children's Mathematics: Cognitively Guided Instruction.* Portsmouth, NH: Heinemann.

Cobb, Paul, and Heinrich Bauersfeld (Eds.). (1995). *The Emergence of*

Mathematical Meaning: Interaction in Classroom Cultures. Hillsdale, NJ: Erlbaum.

Cromer, R. F. (1971). The development of the ability to decenter in time. *British Journal of Psychology, 62*(3), 353–365.

De Corte, Eric, and Lieven Verschaffel (1989). Teaching word problems in the primary school: What research has to say to the teacher. In Brian Greer and Gerry Mulhern (Eds.), *New Directions in Mathematics Education.* London: Routledge.

Dehaene, Stanislas (1997). *The Number Sense: How the Mind Creates Mathematics.* New York: Oxford University Press.

Devlin, Keith (1997). *Mathematics: The Science of Patterns.* New York: Scientific American.

Devlin, Keith (2000). *The Math Gene.* New York: Basic Books.

Donaldson, Margaret (1978). *Children's Minds.* London: Fontana.

Easley, J. (1983). A Japanese approach to arithmetic. *For the Learning of Mathematics, 3,* 8–14.

Field, Hartry (1980). *Science Without Numbers: A Defence of Nominalism.* London: Blackwell.

Field, Hartry (1989). *Realism, Mathematics, and Modality.* London: Blackwell.

Fosnot, Catherine Twomey (Ed.). (1995). *Constructivism: Theory, Perspective, and Practice.* New York: Teachers College Press.

Gelman, Rochel (1979). Preschool thought. *American Psychologist, 34*(10), 900–905.

Gelman, Rochel, and C. R. Gallistel (1978). *The Child's Understanding of Number.* Cambridge, MA: Harvard University Press.

Ginsburg, Herbert P., and Barbara S. Allardice (1984). Children's difficulties with school mathematics. In Barbara Rogoff and Jean Lave (Eds.), *Everyday Cognition: Its Development in Social Context.* Cambridge, MA: Harvard University Press.

Greer, Brian, and Gerry Mulhern (Eds.). (1989). *New Directions in Mathematics Education.* London: Routledge.

Harris, Roy (1995). *Signs of Writing.* London: Routledge.

Hodges, Andrew (1985). *The Enigma of Intelligence.* London: Unwin.

Holmes, Deborah L., and Frederick J. Morrison (1979). *The Child: An Introduction to Developmental Psychology.* Monterey, CA: Brooks/Cole.

Hughes, Martin (1986). *Children and Number: Difficulties in Learning Mathematics.* London: Blackwell.

Hurford, James R. (1987). *Language and Number.* Oxford: Blackwell.

Huttenlocher, Janellen, Nancy C. Jordan, and Susan Cohen Levine (1994). A mental model for early arithmetic. *Journal of Experimental Psychology: General, 123*(3), 284–296.

Kamii, Constance (1985). *Young Children Reinvent Arithmetic: Implications of*

Piaget's Theory. New York: Teachers College Press.

Kamii, Constance (1989). *Young Children Continue to Reinvent Arithmetic, 2nd Grade: Implications of Piaget's Theory*. New York: Teachers College Press.

Kamii, Constance (1994). *Young Children Continue to Reinvent Arithmetic, 3rd Grade: Implications of Piaget's Theory*. New York: Teachers College Press.

Kamii, Constance (2000). *Young Children Reinvent Arithmetic: Implications of Piaget's Theory* (2nd Ed.). New York: Teachers College Press.

Kamii, Constance, and Ann Dominick (1998). The harmful effects of algorithms in grades 1–4. In Lorna J. Morrow and Margaret J. Kenney (Eds.), *The Teaching and Learning of Algorithms in School Mathematics, 1998 Yearbook*. Reston, VA: National Council of Teachers of Mathematics.

Kline, Morris (1980). *Mathematics: The Loss of Certainty*. New York: Oxford University Press.

Lakoff, George (1987). *Women, Fire, and Dangerous Things: What Categories Reveal About the Mind*. Chicago: University of Chicago Press.

Lave, Jean, Michael Murtaugh, and Olivia de la Rocha (1984). The dialectic of arithmetic in grocery shopping. In Barbara Rogoff and Jean Lave (Eds.), *Everyday Cognition: Its Development in Social Context*. Cambridge, MA: Harvard University Press.

Mandler, George, and B. J. Shebo (1982). Subitizing: An analysis of its component processes. *Journal of Experimental Psychology: General, 111*, 1–21.

Mangan, Clare (1989). Multiplication and division as models of situations: What research has to say to the teacher. In Brian Greer and Gerry Mulhern (Eds.), *New Directions in Mathematics Education*. London: Routledge.

McNeill, Daniel, and Paul Freiberger. (1993). *Fuzzy Logic*. New York: Touchstone.

Mulhern, Gerry (1989). Between the ears: Making inferences about internal processes. In Brian Greer and Gerry Mulhern (Eds.), *New Directions in Mathematics Education*. London: Routledge.

Nagel, Thomas (1986). *The View from Nowhere*. Oxford: Oxford University Press.

Nelson, Katherine (1985). *Making Sense: Development of Meaning in Early Childhood*. New York: Academic Press.

Olson, David R. (1970). *Cognitive Development: The Child's Acquisition of Diagonality*. New York: Academic Press.

Olson, David R. (1994). *The World on Paper: The Conceptual and Cognitive Implications of Writing and Reading*. Cambridge: Cambridge University Press.

Popper, Karl R. (1972). *Objective Knowledge: An Evolutionary Approach*. Oxford: Clarendon.

Popper, Karl R. (1976). *Unended Quest: An Intellectual Autobiography*. London: Fontana/Collins.

Rosch, Eleanor, and B. B. Lloyd (1978). *Cognition and Categorization*. Hillsdale, NJ: Erlbaum.

Rotman, Brian (1987). *Signifying Nothing: The Semiotics of Zero.* London: Macmillan.

Saxe, Geoffrey B. (1991). *Culture and Cognitive Development: Studies in Mathematical Understanding.* Hillsdale, NJ: Erlbaum.

Senner, Wayne (Ed.). (1989). *The Origins of Writing.* Lincoln: University of Nebraska Press.

Smith, Frank (1988). *Joining the Literacy Club.* New York: Teachers College Press.

Smith, Frank (1990). *to think.* New York: Teachers College Press.

Smith, Frank (1994). *Writing and the Writer* (2nd Ed.). Hillsdale, NJ: Erlbaum.

Smith, Frank (1998). *The Book of Learning and Forgetting.* New York: Teachers College Press.

Smith, Frank (1999). Why systematic phonics and phonemic awareness instruction constitute an educational hazard. *Language Arts, 77*(2), 150–157.

Smith, Frank (2001). Just a matter of time. *Phi Delta Kappan, 82*(8), 572–576.

Smith, Karan B. (2000). Effects of a cooperative teaching approach on math anxiety in beginning algebra. *Focus on Learning Problems in Mathematics, 22*(2), 1–17.

Tsamir, Pessia, Ruth Sheffer, and Dina Tirosh (2000). Intuitions and undefined operations: The cases of division by zero. *Focus on Learning Problems in Mathematics, 22*(1), 1–16.

Walkerdine, Valerie (1982). From context to text: A psychosemiotic approach to abstract thought. In M. Beveridge (Ed.), *Children Thinking Through Language.* London: Arnold.

Walkerdine, Valerie (1988). *The Mastery of Reason.* London: Routledge.

Wood, David (1988). *How Children Think and Learn.* Oxford: Blackwell.

Woodworth, Robert S., and Harold Schlosberg (1954). *Experimental Psychology.* New York: Holt, Rinehart & Winston.

Name Index

Subject Index

About the Author

Frank Smith was a reporter, editor, and novelist before beginning his formal research into language, thinking, and learning. He gained his Ph.D. at the Center for Cognitive Studies at Harvard University and has been a professor at the Ontario Institute for Studies in Education, the University of Toronto, the University of Victoria, British Columbia, and the University of Witwatersrand, South Africa. He lives on Vancouver Island, Canada. Frank Smith has published over twenty books and many articles on topics central to education. He has spoken at educational conferences and worked with teachers and students in Africa, North and South America, Southeast Asia, Australasia, and Europe.